PAY ATTENTION

PAY ATTENTION

The testimony of one man's salvation.

Hebrews 13-2, "Be not forgetful to entertain strangers: for thereby some have entertained angels unawares."

BILL DONAHUE

XULON PRESS

Xulon Press
2301 Lucien Way #415
Maitland, FL 32751
407.339.4217
www.xulonpress.com

Unless otherwise indicated, Scripture quotations taken from the King James Version (KJV) – *public domain.*

Scripture quotations taken from the Holy Bible, New International Version (NIV). Copyright © 1973, 1978, 1984, 2011 by Biblica, Inc.™. Used by permission. All rights reserved.

Paperback ISBN-13: 978-1-6628-1327-6

Ebook ISBN-13: 978-1-6628-1328-3

DEDICATION

THIS WORK IS DEDICATED TO EVERYONE mentioned in it because you have been a part of my testimony, and without you, I would not have the close relationship to God that I now enjoy every day of my life. Most of all, to my wife Sheila Joe for her understanding of God and leading me to the path and the people who helped me along the way in my journey to find and accept Jesus Christ as my personal Savior. Pastor Chuck Bigler is near and dear to me as he taught me so very much and enabled me to make the discision to accept Christ as my Savior. He is a dear friend, and we share a bond no one else will understand. Pastor Andy Ohman has also been a huge influence on my spiritual journey, and I thank him for his guidance. Jeremy and Cheryl Herman are great friends and were both instrumental in getting this book into print. Their encouragement and participation, along with Sheila Joe's really made this book happen. Our Friday night Bible Study during the writing process provided oversight and gave me the persistence needed to finish and publish this work.

To all mentioned here, I thank you.
Bill Donahue

CONTENTS

Getting Started
PAY ATTENTION: WHO, WHAT, WHERE, WHEN AND WHY

OK, ITS 11:30 A.M. ON FRIDAY, MARCH 15, 2019. I am in my office at the RE/MAX Building in Pueblo West, Colorado, at my desk that has been my work home for almost twenty years now. I have been thinking about writing a book for about a year, and here I am finally doing it. I guess the way to start the process is to sit down at the computer and just start typing, so that is what I am doing. This is to be a book about the who, when, what, where, and why of my relationship with Jesus Christ, my Savior. It is an amazing story, I am told, really a miraculous happening, or at least the very few people I have shared it with seem to think so. Thus, the encouragement and planting of the seed to write this book.

THE WHO? I was never one to think much about these things, Bibles, books, God, angels, church, or anything else spiritual throughout my lifetime. I didn't know or care if it even existed. Oh, I believed in God, and I thought that was enough. Sure I prayed, but only when I was in trouble, about to be in trouble, or wanted something for myself. Mostly, I scolded God when life didn't go my way or something I deemed to be bad happened. Looking back, I guess deep down inside, I knew He was there. Kind of that shadow you didn't really see, that wind that came from and went to nowhere, the reflection in a pond, revealing something that is there, but it's not where or what my mind thought it was. At the time this all started, I was almost done in life; I was a hard-core alcoholic and had been for many years by then. The booze was really taking hold by now and the wear and tear it takes on one's body and mind was showing on mine. I did not know it, but apparently God did, and He was not done with me just yet.

THE WHAT is salvation: yours, mine, anyone's, everyone's. This book is about how one man, about as much the normal American as can be, came to believe in God, really believe, in my heart in a power much greater than any other anywhere at any time. This is how I accepted Jesus Christ as my personal savior. I was like so many others, kind of believed but nowhere near a practicing Christian by any measure. I was a nice enough fellow but a high functioning alcoholic, upper middle class, frustrated with many things in my life. Life at this point was simply hard. I had been through a divorce many years before, recently been through bankruptcy, and both Glenna, my wife at the time, and myself were deep into our addiction to alcohol. We were both slowly dying.

The disintegration of our bodies had begun; a lack of sleep, poor diet, constant injuries from trips and falls, and mental problems all reared their ugly heads. She was much worse off than I was and had begun the downhill slope to death, very ill. The trip that starts the story was a solo Fourth of July trip. Normally Glenna was there, holidays being a big part of our drinking lifestyle, but there was no big party this time, an escape from it all for me was the theme of the journey. This time she was too ill to go up to our high-altitude cabin, let alone do the work or even stay sober enough to be present. In addition to alcoholism, she was suffering from its effects: diabetes, pancreatitis, diverticulitis, as well as having been injured from the slip of a knife while slicing a lime. We had been told many times that if we, she particularly, did not stop drinking, we would die, and she did pass away in June 2016 from acute alcoholism. She will always be a part of this story as she lived in the nightmare of addiction with me.

Denial lived at our house, and misery was our unintended guest. So, this is the story looking back on how I believe Jesus Christ had been there in my life all along, looking for a way to bring me to Him and for Him to enter my heart and save me. As for Glenna, I believe God protected her from more pain and misery by taking her home to heaven and in the process saved me from the same fate. God's Word tells me He works in mysterious ways, and my evidence list proves it. My list is full of things that have happened in my life before and after my salvation that prove the existence of God in my own mind, and this one is high on that list. I was not looking for anything at that time in the way of a solution. A huge spiritual awakening was about to happen to me in a very unusual way and I didn't even know it.

THE WHERE? Winfield, Colorado, is a beautiful, almost deserted ghost town located in Chaffe County in the heart of the beautiful Colorado Rocky Mountains. It truly is wilderness like the ones mentioned in the Bible nearly 300 times: no phone, TV, or internet to occupy the mind, just clean air beautiful scenery and the powerful sounds of nature. I have always said, "It is where God goes when He goes to the mountains." During the late 1800s when mining was the name of the game in Colorado, it was a hustling, bustling place. Founded in the 1860s as Florence, then with a name change in 1881, it became Lucknow and land was free to anyone who would build on the

50 x 100 foot lots. At some point along the way Winfield was adopted and remains the name today.

Reaching its heyday in the early 1890s when the price of silver was high, the population peaked at around 1,500 souls. The small town supported three saloons, three stores, two hotels, a boarding house, a post office, a school, and both a smelter and a concentrator. Unofficially, there was a still and a brothel jointly conducting a banner business as well. Much of the old relics are visible today, along with a few of the original cabins. The mining came to an end in the early 1900s, and the thriving metropolis withered and died along with the industry that had given it life. One can still see many relics of the mining boom. I can see, smell, and hear the goings on of life at that time when I let my mind take the curve into easy imagination. I always thought I was born 100 years too late, so it is a short trip for me. In short, it was a wonderful setting for what was about to happen in my world. And I pray, in yours.

Winfield Colorado in fall, a beautiful place.

THE WHEN? Friday, July 5, 2013, was the day my fifty three year old life began to change forever, not all at once but gradually over the next three and a half years. Up until about eight years before, I had been the golden boy, at least by my own standards. I remember thinking as a young man, "If I can only earn $100,000 a year, I would be rich." I think I held onto that way of thinking way too long, all about the money. I felt I had done well and always succeeded at whatever I tried to accomplish. I worked hard, had the best jobs, got the good promotions, started and ran my own business. I had sold the business and made some big money back in 1998, more than I ever thought possible for me. Then I started a Real Estate career and became one of the top agents in Pueblo County. I made lots of money and enjoyed a big house, boat on the lake, cabin in the mountains, travel at will, lots of toys, parties, and a lifestyle that included a lot of alcohol. I even had Glenna retire from her great job because we didn't need the money. I had been very successful at life, at least in my own opinion. Sure, there had been small setbacks, but nothing that I could not handle and overcome. After all, I was in charge, right? Wrong!

THE WHY? The most important factor in this whole thing is the why. I am no biblical scholar or theologian by any means. I am a new Christian on fire for the Lord, wanting to overcome all the many reasons not to write this. I have only shared my testimony with very few people as I am reluctant to tell it for fear I might be considered crazy. Telling anyone that I was a full-blown alcoholic and had experienced a spiritual awakening in such a bizarre fashion all in the same sentence would certainly make me think the storyteller had lost it, not found it. Now as I read and learn the Word of God, I feel an overwhelming desire to share my testimony because the Bible tells me I must. *All Bible verses are from King James Bible unless otherwise noted.* Matthew

28:19-20 says, *"Go ye therefore, and teach all nations, baptizing them in the name of the Father, and of the Son, and of the Holy Ghost."* Not to mention I received encouragement from my lovely wife (Sheila Joe), my Bible study friends (The Hermans), Pastor Andy's sermons, and the inability to get this out of my heart. When I let it slosh over the sides, I feel good about it, so why not just pour it out in this book? If one single person can read this and move even one step closer to Jesus Christ, or Christ Jesus as it may be, then it is a successful endeavor. Glory to God.

I invite you to join me in my journey to recognize, find, and accept Jesus Christ as my Savior. I am learning to *Pay Attention*; *you* can too. Proverbs 16:3 says, *"Commit thy works unto the Lord, and thy thoughts shall be established."*

The Author where it all started on the mountain. Please note all the pictures in this book were taken by various people at various times not for this book but as this testimony unfolded over time. They are less than perfect but do give a true look into my journey.

Chapter 1
THE INDIAN

I HAD JUST RETURNED FROM THE FOURTH of July ritual started a decade ago. A new American flag was planted on Winfield Peak every year in honor of our country's birthday. On the copper flagpole, I put the name of a friend or family member who was struggling in life; perhaps illness or disaster had struck them. The names were etched into the pole among the previous ones, then the pole was used again the following year. A picture snapped at the peak and sent to them telling about the flag flying in their honor that year on the peak was the tradition. A lift me up for the chosen person was the intention. Then the flag would be retrieved in the fall, cased, and sent to the honoree or the family.

Bill on the peak and the flag placed for a good friend Effie Crider.

1

The annual trip was cold, just above freezing this time of year at timberline. Beautiful, lush, and green, the plants and trees just bursting with new growth were wet and hanging low to the ground. The sound of the runoff roared like a lion down the valley. The morning clouds laid in the valley at the 12,000-foot level like a layer of cotton separating the lush valley floor and the rocky peaks where the sun rays broke through. God's beauty showed through in the white snow laying in the high crevasses on the sheer rock faces. Everything was wet first thing, and by the time I got started, my pant legs were soaked, along with my boots from the dew on the tall grass.

The first part of the trip is by ATV, about an hour's ride to my timberline parking spot. Then the zig-zag hike of about two hours would begin. It was quiet, and as I emerged from the clouds just above timberline, the sun was bright and warm at the summit when I finally reached it. Then I planted the flag, did a photo shoot, and took some time to soak it all in and of course have a nip from my flask. Then I began the return trip back down the steep, narrow trail and ride back to the cabin to rest and have refreshments. It was a proud walk each year, spent thinking about the person whose name I put on the pole. It was a good thing, like helping an old lady across a busy street. It was intended to be a challenge met head on and conquered once again.

On the way back to the valley floor, I had stopped in the usual spot to shift my ride from climb mode, into take it on home mode. Some sort of movement caught my eye to the left, a deer or an elk? No, standing about thirty yards away in a shadow, I saw an Indian standing motionless now. His dark eyes glared at me, no expression on his face. I nodded a friendly mountain-man nod his way. He gave no reaction, so I moved on. Giving it a little thought, he must have wandered away from a mountain man rendezvous up in the big meadow.

Back at the cabin, I was ready to relax. There is nothing like a cold drink after a job well done in the Colorado high country on a warm, mid-summer morning after a seven-hour adventure. I was about to do what I always did after placing the flag on Winfield Peak, get in my deck chair, boots off, slippers on, cold drink in hand, and spotting scope in place to look at the awesome site I had created this fine morning. Sitting back on the deck to admire my own handy work, the flag on the peak would be my view. I saw movement down the road in front of me, about 400 yards away, but moving toward me. I was not sure why, but whatever was heading my way made me feel just a little bit nervous, not afraid, but that feeling a person might get when they are about to go off the high board or pet a snake.

There were people all around. I had seen campers, hikers, and fellow mountain climbers all morning. It was a holiday weekend, so it was a busy place. This unknown shape was something different; I could feel it deep down inside. As the unknown moved closer, 300 yards now, it was moving quickly. I was able to make out the form and the color. It was a man, but it was different somehow. I had only been in my seat a few minutes, one boot off, when I first made out who it was.

It was that Indian I had seen just up the road a short time before. I thought, *Wow, this fellow is really moving.* He had covered more than a mile and a half from where I saw him last up on the mountain and done it in the fifteen minutes it took me to get back and get situated for my flag viewing ritual. It took him about half the normal time. I was still getting my second boot off as I watched him approach. He was letting no moss grow on him; he was on a mission and headed right at me.

Now less than 100 yards away and almost to the turn going down the mountain, he was still moving at a more than quick pace. Surely, he would veer to his right and disappear over the horizon never to be seen again. At least he would pass by me; I would be off the hook. When he got to the turn and passed it heading up the road that passes the cabin driveway and goes up past the old cemetery, that nervous feeling in the pit of my stomach I had a minute ago was quickly becoming a defensive feeling. There was no real reason for my feeling, as I still had my pistol on my belt from the hike and after all, I was afraid of nothing, man nor beast. So why did I feel a threat? I do not know, but I did, and my brain was telling me to put my guard up against whatever was heading my way.

I sensed power and felt like a sheep before a lion, like I could mount no real defense should it become necessary. He drew closer. Now only forty yards away, I spoke to myself silently, *He will go right on past like so many, who go up the road. They look over, wave, or smile and take a moment to admire our beautiful log cabin and then move on.* The American and Colorado flags flying proudly, and the green metal roof make "Ranger Station" a natural assumption.

Some will pause and motion that they would like help, directions, or distance to the cemetery just a quarter mile up the hill. Very few will approach with no permission, even if it's just a glance and a head gesture.

By now my attention was focused on him like a laser beam. He stopped, center of the driveway, quickly turned his head, and looked directly at me with the same glare I had seen a short time before. Now I knew he was looking for me. We were eyeball to eyeball locked in a stare, and we both knew things were about to get up close and personal. He moved like an athlete, strong, powerful, and confident. I had my boots off but no slippers on yet as he approached. As soon as he turned and took one large step in my direction, my heart rate went through the roof as if getting ready for one my adolescent bar fights.

My fists began to clench, and my mind began to plot. I had always been one to meet any challenge head on, so while he began to move in my direction, I stood up and headed toward him as well. He took large, quick steps and made a bee line for the front of the deck, not the stairs leading up to the deck but a place where we would be separated by the railing with me standing two feet higher than him. I was headed for the stairs, so I could go down them and meet him on even ground, but he beat me to his place. He spoke with deep voice, jerking my focus to my left, and causing me to turn and face him only three feet away. Now what?

I focused on him. At this close range, my mind analyzed what my eyes saw. Time seemed to come to a sudden stop. He was tall and thin with a clean, leather-looking face cooked by the hot sun and burned by the wind for untold years. His hair was long and dark, with strands of gray, and tied back with a beaded leather headband holding some large neatly arranged feathers. The buckskins he wore looked well constructed and well worn. The shirt was long like a mid-leg skirt and had fringe tails down the back of both long sleeves and around the bottom with a string tie neckline. No beads or decorations could be seen on the buckskins. The pants looked as though they had been on many a hunt and were stained much darker than the shirt. The fringes of the pants ran down both legs on the outer side. Around his neck was a small necklace with a pouch, just the right size for a silver dollar, and he had a piece of rawhide around his waist as a belt with a polished wood buckle. On his left side hung a possibles bag with a flip-over flap to keep rain out.

Decorations of small colorful beads in an intricate pattern covered the neck pouch and the belt bag. The heavy moccasins on his feet looked well used but in good condition and laced up to mid-calf. Later, he brought to my mind the medicine man from *Dances with Wolves*. There were no weapons or bladder for water visible. His black pool deep eyes were glued on me; his stare penetrating me. My fear immediately left, and a great comfort came in its place. Suddenly it seemed more like a great friend was standing before me, I felt protected now, safe. Looking back, Hebrews 13:2 says, *"Be not forgetful to entertain strangers: for thereby some have entertained angels unawares."*

"I am thirsty; do you have anything to drink?"

His voice rumbled out in broken English like you have all heard in old *John Wayne* movies. I must have felt the need to serve him even though he was a stranger, I responded, I have water, beer, whiskey and ...

He interrupted. "I like whiskey" he growled.

I knew there was a half a bottle of Crown Royal on the table inside. I raised my finger in the air, nodded in his direction, but said nothing. I walked in the door and poured a tumbler more than half full and headed back to my guest. I lowered the glass over the railing down in front of him, holding it by the top rim. He reached up, grabbed it by the bottom, swirled it in the sun, and looked at it with disdain on his face, and downed it in one gulp still holding it by the bottom. The glass was placed on the railing, upside down, and still there was no expression or reaction on his stern face. It was as if the strong liquor was nothing more than water; perhaps it was. Then, silence, a long edgy silence ensued, when I had to speak, Come up and sit, rest, but it elicited no response. I saw my camera nearby and asked if I could take his picture, really to just break the quiet.

"*No*," he said, fast and firm. "It steals the spirit." Silence again, all the while, eye contact was as constant as I could stand. I had to get a conversation started somehow, right?

I asked, "What is your name?" He seemed to think about it a few moments, like perhaps he had more than one name on the tip of his tongue. "Charlie Jones" was the reply. The given name did not ring true with me, so I pressed him a bit. That is not your name; that is like Bob Smith or something. Finally, a conversation began. "My real name is *Managua*" he said loud and proud. "Many people have trouble saying it, so I go by Charlie Jones or C.J.". He extended no hand as a man-to-man greeting, so I didn't either.

Where are you from? What I was asking is, where are you *from*, as in Denver, Chicago, Los Angeles, you know *from*?

"I started in Iron City this morning" he shot back. Now I know that Iron City is at least twenty-two miles away as the crow flies, and there are no roads between here and there, only a network of high mountain trails, some marked and some unmarked and only known to locals and serious hikers. It would be necessary to cross the continental divide twice following those trails. It seemed an impossible task on foot. It was around 11:00 a.m. now, so did he start in the dark? I saw no head lamp, and these are steep, rough, rocky mountain trails. Two miles an hour would be an incredible pace, and that would be at least a full days' hike for an experienced mountain hiker with all the right gear and in Olympic-style physical condition. My next question seemed obvious. How did he get here?

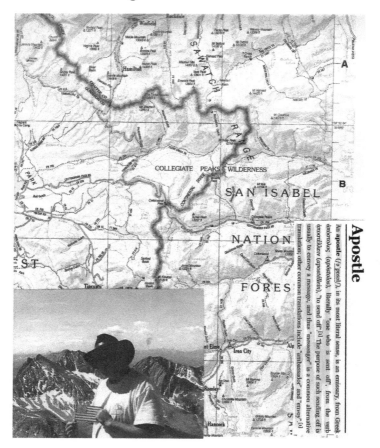

Bill with the Three Apostles in the background and Charlies route from Iron City to Winfield.

I know these mountains well and have hiked most of the trails at one time or another, so I thought this as something of a test. His answer was 100 percent correct. His description of how he got from Iron City to Winfield could have only been recited by someone who had just done it or spent some time tracing and memorizing maps. It included forest service trail numbers, described if it were an incline or decent, landmarks that were seen from the trail and included one trail that is not on any maps but is a local secret of sorts. Having passed that test and satisfying me that he had made the journey just as described, in what had to be some sort of record time, I had to wonder why anyone would make that trip with such an incredible sense of urgency? It had to take the fun out of it for sure. By now, I was feeling good about his presence. It seemed a bit strange, but I was extremely interested in finding out all about this fellow. I remember thinking I would be able to get him up on the deck for a sit in the shade and perhaps a cold one and a long talk. I had leaned on the deck railing, so our faces were much closer now, and I was really soaking in the appearance, he looked like an Indian to me. I asked, what are you doing here?

His face became very stern, then his rough voice broke his silence, "I roam from ancient cemetery to ancient cemetery." Then he leaned in *very close*; he may have taken a step. His face was close enough to mine that it made me uncomfortable, I could smell his breath and see the sweat beaded up on his face, his deep black eyes captured me. I somehow wanted to move but could not.

No pictures allowed; they steal the spirit.

"You *will* be surprised what you *can* find there, *if you Pay Attention!*" he warned, drawing back quickly. The words were spoken like a command and not a request. I was not sure what these words meant at the time, but I was completely sure they were especially important, as though great wisdom had just been spoken. Again, he fell silent. I think I fell back on my unconscious habit of just saying something when feeling like the air was just too calm in a conversation. Again, not feeling so sure of myself, I wanted to engage or run away. However, I was drawn to find out more, so I spoke. Some humor perhaps, would lighten the moment.

I asked, So, how are you going to pay for your drink? Adding a small smile to test his reaction. As it had been up to this point his face was stern.

"I have nothing, nothing to offer" he said, again, that glare. After a long silent pause, "No," he spoke, "I do have something." He did not look but reached up with one hand, pinched the sides of the small pouch hanging around his neck like a small coin pouch my grandma had, forcing it to open at the top. Turning it over to cause the contents to drop into his hand and clasping the contents in his tight fist, he let go of the pouch. Then calmly reaching up, palm down, his hand opened, careful not to drop the prize. Then almost slapping it against the weathered wood railing like a coin on a bar and pulling away his weathered hand revealed the proposed payment, two silver rings, one larger than the other, perhaps wedding bands. Recognizing these were far more valuable than the transaction deserved, *"too much"* crossed my lips with a shake of my head. I don't want those.

Leaning in again and with his attention-grabbing glare, "Yes you do," came his response. Like he knew I wanted them just as much as I knew I wanted them.

"That is too much" I said as I turned away, again not knowing why, except that because deep down, I knew he was right; I did want them. Turning quickly to the door and almost rushing inside, I grabbed the bottle of Crown Royal and a twenty from my money clip. It must have seemed odd because as I handed the half full bottle and the twenty over the rail for him to take, I noticed a small reaction from him. Not from surprise but as though he was pleased and knew exactly what I had in mind. For the first time I saw the corners of his lips turn up ever so slightly, a smile, his head tilting slightly as though to look at the amount remaining in the bottle. I thought, now we are getting somewhere. As my hands returned over the railing and sensing his approval, the rings were scooped into my left hand by my right. I wanted them a lot, and now they were mine.

I slowly opened my hand to take a closer look at my new treasure but was careful not to show I was too excited. *These are the real thing* ran through my mind. The rings were heavy looking, and each one showed some wear and tear, probably expensive. It hit me, these were not laying in the trail, and he did not look like a mall shopper, for sure. Could they be stolen? I knew they were not stolen but felt that I needed to know just the same.

Next question, where did you get these?

His eyes squinted "I found them in Iron City, at the ancient cemetery there, at the base of a headstone. He went on, "A hole had been dug right in front of this headstone. It looked fresh and loosely covered, and I wanted to see what the hole contained so, I dug it up," he explained. "At the bottom of the small hole, I found the rings." Back to his emotionless stare.

I asked with my voice more than just a little shaky, What was the *name* on the headstone?

I was now very afraid as I know there was a headstone in the Iron City Cemetery that had a special meaning to me. Again, not sure why. My mind flashed back many years, to the spot where the headstone stood, at least twenty-two years I had been visiting that spot whenever nearby, the name. What was the name? It took a few moments for it to come to me, it had been a while since my last trip there. At the same moment, an image of the mysterious headstone appeared in my mind, he spoke the name, "Hallie," was all he said.

I knew it was one and the same, and a chill ran through my body. Now, somehow this whole chance meeting became not just chance, but some vision of destiny and I most certainly was *Paying Attention.*

Hallie Dannenhauer was a young girl when she died back in 1893, at about three and a half years old. Oddly enough the same year repeal of the Sherman Silver purchase act brought certain death to silver mining and to the towns built around it, she passed away with the silver boom and the era. Upon repeal of this act, silver prices dropped from $1.00 an ounce to a mere 60 cents, spelling doom for the silver mines in the district, a nail in the coffin of places like Iron City and Winfield, the beginning of their fade into history. Now my first visit to Iron City had been by chance, with my wife at the time, Glenna. Then newlyweds, we had made nearby St. Elmo our destination for the day.

Hallie's headstone in the Iron City cemetery.

One of our passions was mountain travel and especially exploring the old cemeteries found in old ghost towns. The only cemetery nearby was Iron City where many locals were buried back in its heyday. On my first visit there in about 1991, I jumped out of the truck, excited to see what we might find, lost treasure perhaps. My attention locked on this particular headstone, seems like there was an unusual beam of light shining through the towering trees like a spotlight right on it, complete with morning mist floating through the beam. Not far away, I made a bee line for it, and as soon as I reached it, my hand just needed to feel it. *Hot*, it was *hot* when it should have been cold. It was a normal spring morning in the high country, low 40s as I recall. For some reason, this stone felt hot to the touch.

I waived Glenna over to confirm or deny its temperature. She touched it, and she drew back her bare hand at the coldness of it. She looked at me, making a "You are crazy" motion with her finger near her forehead. I went back several times that day, and it was hot each time. Not burn you hot but a soothing, warm fire, kind of hot. Over a dozen times I had been back there over the years, always stopping in to test the mystery of the hot headstone, it never failed-hot to me, cold to others. I never knew why or made any connection to this place, name, family, or story. Now suddenly, it had meaning, but what meaning? I had no idea, but I knew it had meaning. As soon as the name crossed his lips, I knew I would be returning there to see this hole for myself and to test the mystery one more time. And soon.

The silence was back as I gathered my thoughts, it seemed our conversation was over. He looked at the money and made a small shoulder shrug as if it was a waste of time to even own it. He folded the twenty as small as possible and squeezing the neck pouch open again and placed it inside. Lifting the flap on his hip pouch, he dropped the whiskey in, closed the flap and looking again at my eyes with his glare he said, "Good trade."

He then broke his eye contact with confidence, turned and walked, again with purpose, out of the driveway and up the road toward the cemetery just a quarter mile up. No wave, no goodbye, no glance back, just leaving.

I thought, *I must follow him and see what he does at the cemetery.* I grabbed my slippers, thinking They would be much quicker to get on and sturdy enough for a short walk, I better move fast to keep up. Right? A small spring crosses the road just above my driveway, so it would be easy to see what his wet tracks looked like. I was a good tracker, and I could get a look at the track imprint and the gait, but because of the moccasins, I figured it would be difficult. To follow them up the road would be just luck, but I knew the destination, so I had a chance. Just in case he took a detour through the forest, I would have an advantage and be able to spot him before he spotted me. I slid on my second slipper. Out the driveway I headed to pick up the trail; there were no tracks.

I just watched him walk through the water a few seconds before, but there were no wet tracks to be seen. I looked up the long straight stretch of the road, and there was no movement; he had vanished like the wind. I headed up the road at a pace faster than I thought I could go, still tired and now stiff from the seven-hour hike up to the peak. Putting my hunting skills to work as I moved along, the skills used to find a wounded animal after the shot, quick but thorough, intense, *PAYING ATTENTION.* A quarter of a mile passed quickly at a brisk pace. I thought certainly he would be there, on the bench, in the shadows. Perhaps near the headstone I had placed there in 2016 for my good friend and brother in-law, Dennis Ward, who had passed away after a long battle for life. For a moment I wondered if he had something to do with this, as we were much of the same mind.

Nothing. I waited like I would for any kind of movement or sound in an animal down situation, still nothing. No sign. He had to be nearby; I could feel it, like I was being watched. You know that feeling we all get telling us we are not alone, like becoming the prey in a hunt. Like that loud bump in the night that puts me on high alert. I waited a while, long enough that the adrenalin of the encounter and my breathing rate from the brisk chase had started to fade. Until the pain from the morning climb began to settle in my vintage lower joints.

Now I was reminded of all the broken bones, near misses, and rebuilds I had been through, and for a moment I wondered why I was here, why now? The noises of the valley began to float to me as my attention to this matter faded. Voices, laughter, music, and some distant gunfire echoed through the valley. Hey, Charlie had to of gone right past the A Frame, a cabin just up the road from mine 100 yards or so. There were at least twenty people sitting on the deck, playing horseshoes, drinking beer, and throwing a frisbee. If anyone there had noticed the unusual passerby, then it would at least help the thoughts of having had a dream or a hallucination to be put to bed. I admit they were creeping in by now.

Who was this? Why was he here? What did he say? Even better, what did he want; what does this mean? Was he even here? I walked up to the A frame as usual as not to raise any special notice, and spoke with Cathy, one of the owners. Hey, did you see anyone go by a bit ago? On the road? Nothing but a look of confusion back from her, as I added, dressed like an Indian. It appeared to me the Bloody Mary drinks she loved so much had taken full effect, and she couldn't really provide any information as to what passed by. So, I inquired of the whole bunch, anybody see an Indian walk by? Again, some mumbles, laughs, and some invitations to join the party. And some compliments on how awesome the flag looked up on the peak against the blue mountain sky.

They knew how I liked to party, so I got some grumbles as I made my excuse of pooped out. I headed down the road. Another possibility, Russ, my neighbor down the road sits on his deck and reads *Louis La'mour* most all the time. He was there when I went by on my return trip from the mountain just minutes before my Indian encounter. I better get down there and see if he saw anything, after all he would have been only twenty feet from Charlie when he passed by. Hope he was in a reading mood today. My hopes increased, as I rounded the corner below my cabin some seventy-five yards.

I stretched my neck out like a willing Thanksgiving turkey to get a straight-shot line of sight to Russ's deck as soon as possible. Was he there? I saw his feet first. *Yes*, he was still there. Surely, he would have looked up when someone passed by; he was a friendly sort of fellow and never misses the chance to show it with a meek wave. He was close enough to hear even the soft moccasin clad steps, even if he hadn't looked up. I was excited to question him, but the response up the road made me take a more subtle approach with my good friend, lest he think I was on the bottle or just plain crazy. As casual as possible, given my desperation to find out myself if I had lost it. Good book?

"Uuummmmmm, the usual" came the reply.

So, anything good wander by today, critters, people, lots of folks around. I am thinking there is a rendezvous in the field up the left fork.

"Nothing unusual", he replied.

"No cowboys and Indians, no arrows flying around"?

"Just hikers and bikers." Then he looked back to his book as I headed back up the road with a wave and a See ya later. So, he had not seen Charlie either, and I escaped without giving away my concern about my own sanity. Now what?

OK, I had seen an Indian who was invisible to anyone else and had a brief but powerful conversation with this fellow, or whatever it was. Well, he was gone, and I guess I was glad he was; I could just shut my mouth, tuck it inside with all the other things that were mine alone, those things that were shared with no one else. Now forget it, Bill. Then, I reached into my pocket and felt the rings, I pulled them out and looked at them in the bright sun, evidence. I had way more questions than answers. I knew a trip to Iron City would prove this whole thing was just, well it would prove something, I was sure, right?

The rings given as payment.

Chapter 2
NOW WHAT?

THIS HOLIDAY WEEKEND WAS OVER.
Rolling back down the road, my mind was full of dreams, but reality and the day-to-day grind awaited. I left the rings in Winfield, hoping they would evaporate before my next trip up. Besides, I felt strongly they should stay in the mountains where I was certain they had been for a long, long time. I was back to work, but Charlie Jones was never far from my thoughts. I needed to know more about this whole encounter. I had kept it to myself so far, but the imminent trip to Iron City was really eating at me. It was hard to get away with all the things going on in real life, so it took a couple of weeks to plan the trip back to see exactly what the Hallie's headstone story held.

Was it true, would there be a not so fresh hole to see there at her grave? I was feeling certain it would be a big waste of time to go look, that there would be no hole, and I could just hide the rings away without mention, keep my secret, and forget the entire thing. Glenna, my mother Janet, and I made a day of it. Leaving early from Pueblo West we traveled the 100 miles to Buena Vista and stopped at Jan's Restaurant. We ate breakfast while they both tried to talk me out of the trip to Iron City because it was two creeks south of Clear Creek and would add three hours to the trip to Winfield.

19

Glenna pressed me hard as to why I was being so foolish, but it was easier to take the inevitable punishment than to explain. I know we both wanted to just get to Winfield so we could open a new bottle and drink. I needed to know the answer to my question worse than I needed to feed my addiction, and she had no clue why I was so intense. They got a bit upset with me when I would not change my plan, but of course they didn't know what I knew. It was a quiet drive up the road to Iron City, my standard form of punishment from Glenna was what I call "cold shoulder and jawbone" and boy did I get a dose of it that day from Glenna really; Mom was just along for the ride. At least the scenery was beautiful, green and lush. I enjoyed the ride with anticipation building as we got closer and closer. We got off the main road, circled the lake, and we were there.

I could see the headstone from the road, just like always. I stopped the Hummer, jumped out almost while it was still in motion, and made a mad dash for the Hallie J. Dannenhauer's headstone. There it was, born Aug. 29, 1889, Died Mar. 5, 1893, and the hole, the stinking hole was there, just like Charlie said it would be. I stood there staring at the ground. Now this changed everything; it gave truth to the story Charlie told. It was real. How else could this be?

The hole was six inches deep or so and about the same across, like it was dug by hand, the dirt was in a small pile next to the hole, packed by hand. I could see the outline of his hands where he packed the small mound of dirt. I must have had a stupid look on my face. Glenna pored herself a cocktail at the truck and did the *50 yard mosey* up to the spot, as she approached, and said something like, "What's your problem; never seen a hole before?" I am sure I gave her a scowl rather than to explain. I wondered what had happened since the time she and I did this the first time and enjoyed doing it? I guess it was life. Mom sat this one out. "Seen one, seen them all," she said.

I had seen what I came to see and needed to get out of there. Wait, one more thing: I had to feel the stone. With some degree of anxiety, I slowly reached out my hand. I let it hover over the stone for a moment as if to test and see if I felt warmth radiating out of it. Nope. Closing my eyes as my hand touched the headstone, *cold rock*. For the first time, it was as *cold* as it should be. Why? The previous warmth was like the red light on an old phone indicating a message was waiting, and when the message had been delivered, the light went out, cold. Back down the road, Glenna was in the punish Bill mode.

My mind was racing, full of questions. Both my passengers were mostly asleep or close to it after the 100 questions about the reasons behind the trip and the hole and a full dose of cold shoulder and jawbone. It was a quiet ride, either way, just me and the road and Charlie bouncing around in my head. Who is Managua? Charlie Jones, really? What does that name mean? Where did he come from, before Iron City? Will he come back? Who did the rings belong to? Why were they in the hole? Who put them there? How long had they been there, who was the Hallie J. Dannenhauer family? Did they live here? Where did they come from and when?

Things were worse now. I still had more questions; there had to be an answer as to *why*, but it truly escaped me at this point. I had no clue. I knew there would be a lot of figuring out to do when I got back to my office. I was just starting to understand and use the internet, so research it would be. I could get my daughter, Chelsea, to help. She knew some things about genealogy, and more about the computer. Finally, at the cabin, cocktails in hand and taking effect, I thought it a good idea to share my story with them. Mom dozed off, but Glenna listened with much skepticism. No surprise here; at this point, the tension in our marriage could be, and was, felt by most of our family and friends.

I was a total loner, even when not alone because of it. I could have told her the sky was blue, and she would have found a way to make me feel foolish about thinking it, or at least she would try. I was distant and had my guard up. We both had our own style when drinking. I was brash and critical of the facts; she was mean and angry and critical of everything. The more we drank, the worse the appearance of the ugly was in us both. Addiction is horrible! After the telling of what had happened and how and when it happened, her only reply was, "Someone is trying to tell you something."

She was right. I just was not aware of who it was and what it was at that time because my heart was closed and hard. She went off to bed, mostly out of it, while I did my usual, stay up and drink some more just to numb the pain of life. So much to think about. Much to investigate. I do not recall the rest of that trip, but I am sure it was mildly unpleasant.

Now more than ever, I needed information, so I started asking and looking, starting with the easy questions first. I needed to be careful how and who I asked what, as not to share too much and give away my possible mental delinquency. I do not normally investigate the names of people I meet along the way, but hey, an unusual fellow, an unusual name. I started there. *Managua*, the first and oldest recorded birth record according to the Social Security Administration in the US was on April 15, 1931. It is more a Spanish name, really, as it is the name of the capital of Nicaragua, but that is not what I was looking for, or was it? I found a more profound meaning that seemed to fit and perhaps offer some bit of who?

M—mild and gentle ways
A—angelic, a truly pure heart
N—number 1, make sure to take care of yourself above all others (spiritually?)
A—authentic, real
G—gracious, it shows (Wow)
U—unique, your love of life
A—affectionate, to those that matter most

What could this name mean, Man-Agua? Was it just the name he gave, or was there a deeper meaning? I know now He had delivered a message to me that would enable me to stop drinking alcohol, the man, to water symbolically. Man, to aqua. Agua being a Spanish word meaning water, the same way Managua has the Spanish influence. Also, a reminder of the water birth at the beginning of life perhaps? At the same time reminding me of the spiritual rebirth provided by salvation.

John 3:3-8 says, *"Jesus answered and said unto him, Verily, verily, I say unto thee, except a man be born again, he cannot see the kingdom of God. Nicodemus saith unto him, how can a man be born when he is old? Can he enter the second time into his mother's womb, and be born? Jesus answered, Verily, verily, I say unto thee, except a man be born of water and of the Spirit, he cannot enter into the kingdom of God. That which is born of the flesh is flesh; and that which is born of the Spirit is spirit. Marvel not that I said unto thee, Ye must be born again. The wind bloweth where is listeth, and thou hearest the sound thereof, but canst not tell whence it cometh, and whither it goeth: so is everyone that is born of the Spirit."*

I believe he could and did do this because he was an angel, sent to me in a form I would recognize, understand, and Pay Attention to. I think he was a heaven-sent thing. Well, that seemed to fit the situation and offer some comfort for Managua. Now to Charlie Jones, I had no idea here. maybe it was just an easy-to-remember name. That was the reason given by Charlie Jones that day at the cabin anyway. But why not Bob Smith or John Doe or why not a nickname like Manny? I could make no sense of this at the time.

Later when it came to light, it was a *fall out of my chair moment* at a Friday night Bible study with the Herman's. Jeremy Herman, a friend and brother who has much more Bible knowledge than I do, saw and offered an explanation. It came to him instantly as I told this story. It came in a question, "C.J.: Christ Jesus"? That got my attention for sure. Causing me to think, *why didn't I figure that out?*

Who is Charlie? Where did he come from? I knew the predominant tribe in this area was Ute, "The Mountain People" by their own definition. *Noochee*, meaning "The People" was the word they used to describe themselves. *Yutas* is a Spanish word used to describe the "Ute" or "meat eaters." This Spanish influence caused me to wonder if Managua had somehow migrated into the Ute tribe. Also found were some references to the Utah or "Yutas" word in the Shoshonean dialect that came from "top of the mountain" (from *"Utes, the Mountain People,"* by Jan Petit, published in 1990). It is widely accepted that the tribes name was a result of the "Mormonization of the Ute tribes" reference to mountains and most likely had its beginnings in a verse in the Old Testament. Isaiah 2:2 says, *"And it shall come to pass in the last days, that the mountains of the Lord's house shall be established in the top of the mountains, and shall be exalted above the hills; and all nations shall flow unto it*". Many books have been written about the subject; this one is about something else. Moving on.

Now, all this really did not tell me anything about where Charlie' s origins were, other than to allow me to assume with reasonable certainty, he was probably Ute. Really, I guessed, based on his attire, the area we were in, and the probability that he was not a normal, modern man in an Indian costume. Taking his description of his trip to from Iron City to Winfield more literally, I dug out my old map, looking for any clues which may be contained there. I made notes the day he was at the cabin in an afterthought about his visit. It did not hit me as he spoke about his hike, but then as I realized how correct it was, I grabbed my map to verify.

Up Poplar Gulch from Iron City on Trail No. 1436, and it is *up*, for sure, then down to Cottonwood road No. 344, over to Ptarmigan Trail No. 1444, then up trail No. 306 over the continental divide for the first time. Then up South Texas creek trail No. 417 to North Texas Creek trail No. 416, then up Prospector Gulch trail No. 414 to the Lake Anne Jump, not on the maps, by the way. Over the continental divide for the second time down past the three Apostles, through Hamilton and "Here I am." Yup, that was it, that is how I would do it, as well. I was sure there were clues contained here, but at the time I could only be amazed at how much country had been covered in a short amount of time, about twenty-two miles and how much elevation change, both up and down, had been done. I know from experience, there is plenty of air available up there, but the oxygen content makes it difficult to maintain a normal heart rate. I am still making assumptions on who Charlie is to this day but thinking he is a messenger sent by God, read on.

Hallie J. Dannenhauer, I knew, was a girl "Dau of" Le Van and Agnes Dannenhauer (no space like on the headstone). I knew when she was born and when she passed away, not much really. It seemed to me the headstone was crowded, so why abbreviate? Why shorten Daughter to Dau? Why did they abbreviate the months? I did find out that her mother and father are also buried in Iron City, but there are no records of exactly where they can be located. Now, I wonder if the rings were theirs? Was it like someone wanted to place them there for them but was unable to find their graves, so they were left with Hallie and then delivered to me by Charlie? Why?

Hallie J. Dannenhauer

BIRTH	29 Aug 1889
DEATH	5 Mar 1893 (aged 3)
BURIAL	Iron City Cemetery
	Chaffee County, Colorado, USA
MEMORIAL ID	15093021 · View Source

Gravesite Details Daughter of Agnes and LeVan Dannenhauer

Hallie also had two brothers, born a few years later, that show up in the Denver and Leadville areas in the U.S. census. Glenna and I tried on the rings, and they fit both of us. The opinions of some of the *old timers* in the valley were headstones were hard to come by and very pricey in those days, so when one was needed, the family was forced to take what was on hand (remember, no embalming or refrigeration). It looked like an expensive marker for the era according to the elders in the valley. The mourning family had a lot to say, so the needed words were most likely crowded into place on the marker stone that was available. It may have been an indicator of the family's prosperity. Were they better off financially than most?

Perhaps her father was a shoemaker by trade; many of the same surname had this for a trade. Shoes were in demand as mining could not be accomplished without good boots. Few records exist to confirm or deny the facts as most of the workers were immigrants and had no birth records. Hallie's grandmother, Glenna, yes, the same name as my wife at the time, shows up as an incoming immigrant from Ireland in 1849.

The excitement of the new mysteries at the cabin faded a bit in the next few weeks as nothing new happened other than the possibility of a Charlie sighting during the fall hunting and fishing excursions. I continued to keep the July encounter to myself, other than an occasional ribbing from Glenna. "See any Indians?" she would ask when I came back from fishing. I must admit that I would go *Charlie hunting* especially when at the cabin alone. I would frequently go up to the cemetery just looking for any sign. Then one afternoon, engaged in a conversation of a passerby, the word "Indian" came up. My ears perked up, Indian, what Indian I inquired? Seems this man's cousin and her husband had been in a campfire argument the night before. It was over the Indian she had seen up at the Winfield Cemetery, but only a few feet from both, unseen by him. I asked what he looked like, but this fellow had no idea.

I got the number of the cousin who saw the Indian first-hand. No phone service was available there, so I was forced to wait until the next day when we came home. I called and left a message, leaving a brief description of the reason for my call and my number, two days, no call back, another message, no call back. Four or five days passed, I called, it rang, and she answered. However, as soon as I started to say "Bill Dona ..." CLICK. She did not want to talk to me about an Indian. Leaving a final voicemail to call me should she feel the need to discuss what she had seen, I left her alone.

Glenna continued to deteriorate from the effects of alcohol, and by November she had been caught drinking at work. The place she worked allowed her to keep her job if she got imme-diate treatment, her first try at rehab. Life was hard, but I was in charge, still drinking while visiting her in rehab. I pushed through the remaining months of 2013, dealing with the Parkview Hospital chemical dependency unit (CDU) in Pueblo, along with our continued addiction to alcohol. No snowmobile trips this winter, because we had no time, no money, no desire to go, despite the questions remaining concerning Charlie Jones. Between the last visit to the mountain that fall and the first 2014 visit in May, there were knocked over mailboxes, dented fenders, hospital visits, medical diagnoses, and much booze-driven misery at our house.

The summer of 2014 started like many before it but with a new Ford F-150 in the driveway for Bill. The Hummer had 250,000 miles on it now, and it was time for new wheels. You know that feeling you get when you have a brand-new vehicle to drive, no scratches, no funny smells, no weird sounds, just a nice shinny truck with only the few miles on it that you yourself put there? I wanted to decal the truck with my RE/MAX logo, phone number, and web address as I had done in the past if for no other reason but to make myself the center of attention. It had been a long time since my last new vehicle, and I was proud of my accomplishment. I recall the feeling in my gut when Glenna took it to the liquor store for more Seagram Seven, and when she returned there was a huge dent in the rear quarter panel. Her response to my anger was, "To bad, not my fault someone hit your truck, get over it."

That's just the way things went then. I eventually let it go, kind of, but the dent and my anger were both still there.

Chapter 3
FRIEND TURNING

ON THE FIRST TRIP IN THE YEAR OF our Lord 2014 to *Winfield Willy's Bar and Grill*, as our cabin was named for its continuous open bar and steaks on the grill atmosphere, expectations were high as they were in years past, hoping for a good summer and some relief from the misery of the long winter at home. I was somewhat of a celebrity in the Clear Creek Valley, known for the countless search-and-rescue missions executed by the other self imagined business I ran as a service to all commers, Winfield Search and Rescue. Some thought of me as the mayor of the small berg; anytime there was trouble to be dealt with, repairs to be made, lost hikers to be found, or just general complaining about the Forest Service to be done it seemed, I became involved. I had been the president of the Clear Creek Canyon Historical Society and was always on the board of directors. I had no authority, but these things sure kept me in the limelight, and I loved it. My sidekick, Glenna, was known as Wilderness Woman to the other cabin owners. People liked her but kept her at a distance, mostly because of the unpredictable moods she demonstrated.

I think by now they all waited to see how drunk she was before engaging with her. She was super nice and loving when sober, then a small window of tolerance before it went to her head, but she was no fun when gin and tonic was on board and in charge. We had hats and coats made and handed them out to cabin dwellers as a just for fun thing. That's what we told ourselves. I now think the real motivation was more along the lines of "look at me." I am sure it appeared to those on the outside looking in that things were just as they should be. Putting forth a look and feel of real success was our specialty, we would have conversations about how our decisions would appear to the other cabin owners, things like the cost of the food we served, the grade and quantity of the booze in the cabinet, and on and on. We had to put up a good visual for our fans. In hindsight, it was all one big front. I knew we were in trouble but had no clue what to do to break the cycle.

Glenna was back to work for the same hospital she worked at before her episode, now in a new position. The company owned the rehab unit she had been admitted to, now she was working as a housekeeper in the rehab unit she was admitted to last year. Apparently, she made a good impression with the staff there while gaining her feet in sobriety. I did not know if this was a good thing or not. At least they would keep her sober during the day. Right? I never did have a problem. I drank a little, but no one knew exactly how much, I was sure. When suggested by a friend that I may have a drinking problem, I would always toast, *I will drink to that* and move on. Deep down I knew it was true, but I stayed in a state of denial.

The front we put up for onlookers at home and at the cabin was no more than a thin crust; as soon as we were done "down talking" the same folks we had been laughing with a short time ago and were back at our own cabin alone, then the true us came out along with the strong drinks, cold shoulder and jaw bone, mean looks and sharp tongues. Both our alcoholic personalities emerged, and the misery began. The same held true wherever we found ourselves. Most onlookers thought things were just fine, but the truth was just under the surface. We were angry with each other and out of control with our drinking most of the time, so the trip up the valley to start summer 2014 would be a nice break.

I made my mind up to let the brand-new dented truck episode go as it drove just as nice with or without the dent, but I was planning on hiding the keys for sure. I never really let it go. Each and every time I saw it there, it was like stubbing that sore toe all over again. Each year the first trip is a big one, loaded with supplies for the upcoming summer long party season. A truckload of food, booze, gas, tools, water, clean laundry and parts for anything we could think of, lots of things to carry inside. We left Pueblo West early in the morning and would make it a two day, one night thing. All the attention was on just getting there and keeping her sober for the weekend.

She claimed to be making a real effort at sobriety, but all evidence of her trip through rehab last fall was gone. She had learned in rehab how to drink less, according to her. She thought she had learned some new tricks on how to hide the problem but appeared stupid when she tried it with me. It gave two birds of a feather a new topic to fight about. It takes one to know one. As we bounced up the twelve miles of bumpy road between Highway 24 and Winfield, there was much anticipation as I was not sure we would be able to make it to the cabin. There were other tracks going in that looked a few days old, and I hoped who ever made them had the determination to break the snow drifts, move the trees blocking the road, and provide a track for us all the way up. We would see. At one point just below Beaver City, Glenna pointed her finger with a loud "Look."

My thought was some elk, or a spring bear would be showing itself, so slamming on the brakes and focusing in that same direction to a spot where the still mostly frozen creek made a wide turn. A sandy beach on the outside corner stood out. I was straining to see movement but saw nothing. Turning to her with a look of wonder, I said, What? She looked at me with her own sarcastic smirk.

"Just saw your Indian friend, but he is gone now."

She was a good spotter, so I pushed her, *Really?*

She got me, but now my mind returned to Charlie Jones and the still-lingering thoughts. It brought back all the questions from the year past. The rest of the ride was silent. It was our lucky day; the early travelers had opened the road all the way, and we were able to pull right into the driveway at Winfield Willy's. My tension relieved, the work began: shutters and doors opened to let the old stale air out and the fresh spring air in. The normal procedure began, open up and carry in. Then Glenna would unpack while I started the fires to get the warming started and the other necessities hooked up and turned on.

On about the third trip in the front door with a load of grub in her arms, Glenna's head pointed to a spot next door from the porch as she went past and inquired, "What is that"? I did not see anything there and shrugged my shoulders in her direction. She put down her load, went back to the deck, and did a close up point next to the front door, knob high, like she was afraid it would jump on her if she got to close. "What is that" she asked again? Pointing more closely. I went outside to see for myself, thinking I may need to smash a spider or catch a mouse.

Nope, that was not the case at all. Remember, there is no phone service so the best way to let someone know where you went in case you don't return as planned or when you do plan to return is to leave a note. So that we all know where the note will be located, each cabin has a nail next to the front door. That is the designated note holder so to speak, an old-fashioned tele-graph, if you will. Our nail was one of the old square, hand-pounded nails from the era gone by. About a size 16 common, I think, very rusty and slightly bent. It had probably been there a long time, at least as long as we had owned the cabin. Now this day there was something on the nail. After looking closely, it appeared to be money, a bill, folded up ever so small, *Wait!*

The flashback of what Charlie had done with the twenty I handed him jumped out of my memory. He had folded it ever so small and put it in the pouch hanging around his neck. A clue, it was a clue! Work stopping, I tried to pull the nail out with my fingers first, no go; it took the channel locks, a firm grip, and a hard tug to remove it from its place. Then the task was getting the bill off the nail. It was crammed on real tight, about an inch up the nail from the point end. The point end of the nail was square, so I could not figure out how it may have been driven through the bill, but there it was. I got the bill off the nail and began to unfold it. The bill looked like Swiss cheese; there were so many holes in it from the nail.

But as it unfolded, the denomination became obvious; yes, it was a twenty. After getting it unfolded, it was apparent there was more damage to the center of the bill. It had been cut, like with a knife. *Now,* suddenly, Glenna became real interested in this bill, probably able to tell I was excited to see it. Was Charlie still around? I am not sure if I want him to be or not. Did he spend the winter up here? Where is he now? Outside watching? That feeling of being watched crept back in.

I knew I would not be able to figure it out quickly; cold and dark were on the way, so I went back to work for now. Evening came, and the work came to a slow stop. The bill had been on my mind all day, and I was anxious to look at it more closely. Making a drink and settling in for the night, I began the doctor like examination, magnifying glass in hand. It had thirty-two mostly square holes in it from the tight fold and penetrations about 1/8-inch in size, evenly spaced of course, like a grid. It had been carved for sure, looked like letters about ½-inch in size cut into it in the center, top to bottom and side to side. I flattened it out, turned it over, flipped it around and finally held it up to the light. There it was, I could read it, the words *"Too much,"* had been cut into the bill. Too much?

$20.00 with TO MUCH cut into it.

Those were my words about the silver rings as payment for his drink, too much. Glenna seemed all in on the Indian mystery now and asked a bunch of questions about the original encounter, especially the conversation Charlie and I had that day. I was in the figure it out mode and began to say, "Too much what? Over and over again. She started responding to every repetition with her answer, "Too much drinking" By the end of that evening, after much very serious discussion, we had decided the too much was probably a warning to us both about the problem we both knew we had. At least we would take it that way, no matter how the $20 got there or who put it there.

This was the first time we spoke about Charlie being something of a supernatural delivery man, an omen maybe, a sign. We promised each other we would stop drinking, somehow, someway, we would stop, for one another's sake. She suggested rehab again, but for us both? At least we got along well the rest of the trip due to way less drinking by both of us. It was one of the few times the elephant in the room had been talked about that did not end in an argument, each pointing a finger at the other. The next day, after the wood was split and the oil changed in the generator, I spent a good deal of time just looking for any more clues that could have been left by our friend. Though not wanting to admit it, I could tell Glenna was searching as well. There had to be something more than, *too much.*

Our vows to quit drinking quickly became postponed as we headed home the very next day, had to have one for the road, right? Shortly, they were forgotten completely. Summer went on with all the normal happenings, trips up the mountain to Winfield, busy at work, and of course, the drinking took its normal place and continued as usual if not more intense than ever. By now, drinking had become the predominant thing to us both; it did not matter where we went, what we did, or who we were making plans with. How would we get our fix was the biggest concern; if there was no alcohol, we simply would not go. The most common choice was to stay home and drink or go to the cabin and drink. We had completely stopped doing the things we got so much pleasure from just a few short years ago. This included placing the flag on Winfield Peak. I did not do it in 2014. I am now incredibly sad about this.

My heart was broken later that summer by the phone call from the supervisor at the rehab center. Glenna had been drunk on the job and had been fired for it. The warning had not been heeded, and now the price must be paid. *Too much* was the case. The job loss was huge; we lost her income and our health insurance immediately. In addition, she was now unemployable. Life got ugly at our house. About a month later, I woke up in the night, realizing she was not in bed with me, so I called out. There was no answer, probably drinking in the other room. I went to look, not there, not anywhere. Both cars in the driveway and the front door was locked, but I feared she had wandered away.

I began to panic. Rushing into our bathroom to put my bottoms on and go looking outside, I spotted her. She was laying in the bathtub, on her back, hands crossed across her chest, pale white like she was dead. She had no clothes on, and when I touched her with my heart pounding out of my chest, she was ice cold. My mind told me, "She is dead." She let out a moan at the bright light, letting me know there was still a chance. I grabbed her up with strength that came from somewhere, put her on the bed to wrap her in a blanket.

Then I put her over my shoulder and into my truck and headed to the ER about five minutes away. I pulled in and laid on the horn, went around, jerked her over my shoulder and headed for the door. It seemed like there was a stretcher there where it should be, and people to help me lower her on to it. Yes, she was drunk, but it was much worse this time, I could tell. It was like on TV, they rushed her through the doors with half a dozen medical personnel working on her. I collapsed.

When I came around, I was informed she had been taken to the main hospital with a blood sugar of 1,400. She was clinically dead; her chances of survival were zero. When she had the pancreatitis, I was told her chances were 50/50, if she stopped drinking. The diverticulitis gave her about a 60 percent chance of survival and a 50/50 of a colostomy bag companion for the rest of her life if she stopped drinking. Obviously, she had not stopped drinking. I had never dealt with these odds unless it was imminent. I had to go home, find the paperwork, and prepare myself for the worst. And drink.

At the hospital, life support was deployed, the ICU unit staff was incredible, and, in a few days, she was sitting up and speaking, much to my surprise. She was a medical miracle. No one lives with that level of blood sugar. She should be dead or at the very least have brain damage that would render her a vegetable. And she was alive and sober.

They released her about two weeks later with strict instructions to not consume any alcohol of any kind, a booklet on how to manage her new diabetic condition and a small dose of hope for the future. She had attended some addiction classes during her diabetes training to help her stay on the straight and narrow. The scolding I received concerning my consumption was very unpleasant as well. The doctors gave me a stern warning to eliminate the alcohol from our home, her life, and from mine. That was the warning, or we would both be dead. If she drank, she would die, and her death would be my fault, and my death would be my fault. It seems they put me in charge of both addictions.

Fine, I would cut her off, but I was strong and smart and could handle my own business. Besides, she was the one that was sick, not me. She got better and stayed sober through the fall and into the winter. She did well but losing fifty-five pounds left her a frail 105 pounds. Then through some miracle she got a job offer from a friend of a friend who needed to fill a position with someone who could pee clean, no drug or alcohol use. It was a state job to boot, housekeeping at a nursing home for veterans. It was perfect.

She loved old people, the pay was good, and our benefits were better than before. Not much cabin time that winter, money was tight, and the medical bills were huge. I mostly just stayed home and worked and drank. The winter passed with only one solo trip to the cabin on the snowmobiles to check on things, 2015 would be our year. Recovery?

Chapter 4
FINAL SUMMER

FINALLY, SPRING WAS IN FULL SWING, we had survived another winter, another set of holidays, another birthday for me, and another for her. We were both excited about getting up the mountain and back to God's country. Too much seemed to be sticking, and for Glenna it had become, one is in fact too much. She was a few months sober, her diabetes was under control, and although my addiction was in full swing, we seemed to be getting along much better. Just removing one addiction from our home made a huge difference in day-to-day life. I think we were both trying to rebuild a broken relationship at this point, even to make friends again. Our marriage had died a long time ago; there was love still, but it was just battered and bruised as bad as our bodies from the addiction and all it brought to bear on life. The first trip was much like all the first trips had been, a large load of goods and supplies were loaded in the dented truck, and up the mountain we ventured. This year a much better attitude accompanied us.

The road was particularly rough because we had a lot of snow, meaning lots of mud and it only got bladed occasionally. The pace was slow, and it was bouncy. The rough road tends to give some travelers the tendency to go, you know use the Bunny (our outhouse is named The Bunny, another story in the story).

We were later this spring, the drive up was not in question as to easy arrival, so no pit stop was requested in Buena Vista. On we drove. Upon arrival, Glenna said, "Throw me the Bunny keys"; she needed to go badly. So, I did, and around the corner she disappeared. I started the open-up sequence with the front door and the big shutters, unlock, open, secure, one after the other. When she came back around the corner, she had a stick in her hand, squinting as if to see a small pebble or tiny writing. Holding it out to me, she asked, "Why was this there?"

What is it, and where was it? I inquired.

"Just a stick, stuck in the lock hasp of the Bunny." I did not know, so it was laid aside, and the spring ritual was underway. After the work was done and evening settled in, the deck was the place to be. The view of the peak made me sad about not going last year, but at the same time I was determined to go this year. Who should I fly the flag for this time? I had no idea that it would be the most difficult climb of my life.

My attention drifted to the small stick laying on the railing near where Charlie had placed the rings. It seemed so long ago and was all but just an old memory that really had no meaning except the *too much* cut into the twenty that may have saved her life. I remember looking at her and thinking how proud of her I was for not drinking and how she was getting the glow of life again, the same glow she had when we first laid eyes on each other twenty-four years ago. I was disgusted with myself as I looked down at the drink in my hand, realizing that I was weak, and she was strong. I had let her down so many times. My glow was very dim. Then for no reason at all, I reached out and picked up the stick and brought it closer to get a good look.

It had been sharpened on one end with a knife, not to a sharp point but kind of square point like the nail. Could it be a clue? I needed to find out, so I said, "Let's go inside and take a closer look at this silly stick." Once inside, the generator started and lights on, we plopped in the kitchen because the light was the best at the kitchen table. It did not take long for us to spot the initials carved into the small piece of wood, C.J, carved near what would be the top as it was left in the hasp.

the clue stick with C.J. in it.

It is a clue! We got the twenty, a picture of Hallie's headstone, and the rings out and began to really take a hard look at
them. Markings inside each ring, stamped into the metal indicated the quality of the ring to be high, once again indicating
financial ability in the Dannenhauer family. No real clue that I
could tell so I asked her, where was it?

"In the hasp of the Bunny," she said. We each secured a
flashlight and went to the Bunny for a closer look see. Any new
clues, we wondered? In the dark, with two bright lights doing a
late-night outhouse search, kind of silly, I am thinking. But one
last look inside, and there it was. The trim inside is made from
small aspen trees, just as they came from the forest with all their
natural beauty in place. Near the door on the right side where
the wall meets the ceiling, there it was. On a small broken limb,
a ring, a diamond ring. Really excited to see our treasure, we
returned to the kitchen. It was the engagement ring matching
the smaller ring Charlie had left with me, the same size, same
metal, and very fancy for its era with two large stones, about $3/4$
carat each. The decorations appeared very intricate, again, I
am thinking an expensive ring.

now the full set was in hand.

Why? Why in the Bunny? How? How could it be inside? The Bunny was always locked when we were not there, with a commercial grade Master lock no less. This means Charlie had to put it there last winter before I left after my one trip but while it was still unlocked, or he had a key, unlocked the door, put the ring there, and closed and relocked the door. I went back out to look and see if there could be any other explanation, like the door being lifted off its hinges, pry marks, anything that could give a clue. I found nothing, and looking it all over again with two sets of eyes, Glenna spotted some scratch marks on the wall just below where the ring had been hanging: *PAY ATTETION* (mis spelled), an underline, then, CJ and an M just below. No punctuation, just the letters and the line.

The stick the ring was hanging on and the carving in the wall inside the Bunny.

Oh boy, now he had been there while we were here, or not, and left a written message. Why? We talked most of the night about what it could mean. More clues but no answers. We wondered if we were *PAYING ATTETION* or if some message or special meaning of life were right in front of our faces, but we just could not see it. It was there, on the table before us, yet it was invisible. The meaning escaped us. Matthew 16:25 says, *"For whosoever will save his life shall lose it: and whosoever will lose his life for my sake shall find it."* It was right in front of us, yet we could not even begin to see it. A true mystery at the time.

It was the middle of May now, and spring was springing, things were going well at home, and her birthday was just a week away. How about a gathering at the cabin, a birthday party? She would be fifty-nine. It would not be one of those monumental birthdays, but she was alive and sober. We were getting along well, so I wanted to do something nice for her, a party it would be. It would be Memorial Day to boot, a three day weekend bash.

People from my work were invited, a few family members as well. Lots of seafood and steaks, and lots of booze. It was a definite party atmosphere. We were all having a ball. The ATVs were busy, horseshoes clanged, bonfires crackled, steaks cooked, and music played.

And Glenna drank. I think it was the first time she had tempted fate after the doctors warning of *drink and die I* was oblivious to it all; she was after all an old hand at hiding the addiction. But now, with the diabetes inside and the booze onboard, her system went into shock, and by Sunday morning she was in trouble. Our guests were thrown the keys and asked to lock up; she was loaded in my truck, and down the mountain we came. I was so angry; how could she? There was no point in conversation as she was not capable of words, let alone logic.

Looking back, I wonder, was I? My addiction was in full swing; I never even stopped for a day. The doctor's warning ran through my head, again and again and again. When she dies, "it will be your fault." My heart sank, this *was* my fault. When we got closer to Salida where the closest hospital was, she came to and began to cry and ask for forgiveness from me and from God. She was ready to deal. Looking back, I think Jesus saved her at this moment. Romans 10:13 says, "*For whosoever shall call on the name of the Lord shall be saved.*" The proposed bargain was, I would take her home, she would sober up, and as long she never drank again, God and Glenna were in good standing. After many tears, much frustration, and lots of discussion, I headed home where she slept it off.

A few days passed, and it was plain she had broken her promise to God and to me. I had been told that Alcohol is cunning, baffling, powerful, and patient. It was true. I could not stop her; she had slipped into even a deeper addiction and didn't care. She was fired again, this time for telling her boss to *XXXX* off, probably still drunk and hung over. Her sister Donna came to our house that day to fix things but instead called an ambulance because Glenna was nonresponsive. The EMTs found an empty quart of vodka buried in the outside dumpster; the lid was in Glenna's pocket. Throwing up was the morning ritual for her, a big glob of yellow bile; she rarely made it to the stool. Food would not stay down. June brought another visit to rehab, the same place she had been fired from the year before. I had lost her. The addiction was in charge, and my visits to rehab were nothing more than silence or a fight.

She had lost her will to get or stay sober. I was at a loss. I looked for answers in the Charlie Jones clues and felt they were there, but I could not see them through my own cloud of addiction. Time passed. After her release and more stern warnings, she was home again, physically sober for now. But it was different this time; she was emotionally destroyed by her addiction, mean, calculating, and devious. The glow of life was gone. I knew that the only way I could keep her from drinking would be to hold her hand and slap her when she reached for the bottle; otherwise, how could I possibly stop her? I could not. It was eggshells at home, with little conversation. Life seemed to be in slow motion as June crawled past. There was no joy.

The traditional Fourth of July climb was edging closer, and somehow my brain concluded that if I made the climb and put her name on the flagpole, it could somehow give her, and maybe even me, the strength to stop. Deep down I hoped to see Charlie again on the mountain. There was an answer within him if I could only *Pay Attention*. There had to be a way out. The hardest climb off my life was at hand.

The solo ride from home to the mountain on the third of July 2015 was long and dry. Dry because I was struggling with my own desire to drink, I just would not do it this weekend, like a sacrifice or something. I would put the flag up in the morning, and if there was a God, He would fix things. I was determined. I could feel withdrawal kicking in within an hour or two of leaving home. The true strength of addiction gets revealed when packing the booze, just in case, while being totally committed to stay sober. The flag was ready; a new 3 x 5 American flag mounted on a new copper pole, her name etched in the pole to let God know it was for her, I imagined. She and I had been face-to-face the evening before. I explained why I was heading out and that things were about to change for the better; I would find the answer. Her reaction was a smirk on her lips, a shrug, and a small smile showed through as I am sure she knew she could drink in my absence with no grief. She could tie one on. I was sure she did before I was out of the driveway. It was a long night alone at the cabin. Rain fell on the steel roof, providing a somber mood, and of course the drinks I was not going to drink penetrated my brain. The dark side crept in; would she be alive when I got home? Would I even make it up and back? Did I care? I would be emotionally and physically spent at the starting gate the next morning. Starting before dawn on the Fourth was really because I could not sleep, not because of some noble calling. I was bored, and I needed to go or just get drunk. I chose to roll. On the ATV headed up the road at 4:00 a.m., through the heavy mist of the rain the night before, feeling the cold in my face and every rock in the road, I felt uneasy about the whole thing. Like a big mistake was about to be made, and I was the one making it. The ride to timberline was over now, the hike began, the hard part. The Crown Royal in my thermos called to me, and I answered, just enough to calm my nerves but not so much as to make my steps unsure. One long draw and the relief was in me, and I could feel the effects like a warm fire flowing through my veins. I would be OK now.

The climb begins at timberline, cold and clear, barely above freezing and misty, head lamp on my head pointed up the narrow trial, straight up on one side, straight down on the other, loose and steep, A couple hundred yards up, out of breath and dizzy, leaning on my rock-climbing poles, I realized this was not the best decision I ever made; in fact, it was downright stupid. I had been here before in the dark but not in this condition or in these conditions. Finding a good spot to sit and wait for some sunlight seemed right. It was a small step in the right direction; at least I would be able to see. Avoiding a bigger mistake seemed important.

The trail up to the peak, strait up, strait down.

The trail is a zigzag affair, up one zig, rest, up the next zag, rest, do it again. I managed to get to the peak in one piece. Direct sunlight was the prize because the climb is on the west side and in the shade of the mountain all the way up. The top allows eastern exposure to the sun, and its warmth felt super good. So good, I deserved a small nip as a reward. Without hesitation down it went, I felt better knowing in a few minutes, my friend, alcohol, would be making the decisions. After rearranging the rock that I had piled up to hold the flag, I planted it firmly in its spot and let it unfurl itself in the breeze.

Breathtaking!

It was beautiful. I sat and stared at the tips of 13'ers and 14'ers to the north still snow laden with winter's snow cornice artwork and the bright fresh green of spring on the valley floor. I think I prayed for God to carry out *my* wishes, or I would be angry at Him. My thoughts ran wild. I would have stayed longer, but my friend was running low by now, and I still had to get back down the trail without falling and killing myself. For a second, it seemed that the later may not be so bad. The third switchback is the most traitorous, with rocks, odd shapes and sizes, all loose and on steep angles, lots of ankle traps and moving footholds. It would be real easy to misstep, even stone-cold sober. I was not, and I did, tripping over my own two feet, down I went, leading with my face. I was extremely lucky the mountain caught me; it could have been a 2,000-foot, out-of-control tumble, but it wasn't. Lying there, taking an inventory of the pain I felt, I was sure my face got the worst of it, I could tell by the blood trying to pool up in my eyes. I was head down, so rolling over and sitting up was no simple task on the steep grade; spitting the gravel out of my mouth helped. There was no mirror nearby, so using the braille system, I knew I would live. I got a new smile out of the deal by the feel of a broken front tooth. After regaining my composure, down I came, inch by inch, a slow, painful decent. No Charlie. The flag viewing ritual had no appeal this time, crawling into the cabin came hard, a blank page in my memory is the rest of the day. It was lost. The day after was worse, now looking like I had been in a bar fight and feeling like I had been in a bar fight, physically, and totally ashamed. I avoided all the other cabin dwellers, locked up and headed home with a gut full of impending doom, certain nothing had changed. I was right.

Chapter 5
END OF THE TRAIL

THINGS AT HOME WERE THE SAME OR worse. The rest of the summer drug on with nothing eventful changing. We were both flirting, even teasing disaster. Our overall heath was in a steady decline. Her balance between diabetes and alcohol was a losing battle for sure, and I was beginning to experience the symptoms she had a year ago, sick every day, losing weight like crazy, with no sleep. I spent my nights on the sofa. My drinking was bold and in the open; hers was in the closet and not discussed. By the end of each day, we were both in the haze of addiction.

We were not fighting as much, more just avoiding each other, simple tolerance. I think this can happen in a marriage when both partners just do not care anymore. We made no attempt to go to the cabin, and there was no mention of Charlie, the twenty, too much, the rings, or any other of the topics we were once passionate about. August 15th would be our twenty-fourth wedding anniversary. I do not remember why or how, but we came up with a plan to go to Estes Park for the weekend. It was something we had done before and enjoyed it. We had no real plan for anything special, just a getaway and relief from the misery, I suppose. A drive through Rocky Mountain National Park would be nice, another pastime we enjoyed, drive and spot.

I rented a condo but made sure it was a two bedroom, so we could each have our own space. We were both good with separate bedrooms; intimacy was long gone, and I'm sure we both wanted it to stay that way. The trip was uneventful other than the pretend relationship we had. No, I love you's, no hand holding, she would flash the I love you sign language sign when a picture was snapped but more for the photo op than for me. We were still keeping up the all is well image. We were nice enough, but that is all. Her favorite image had always been the *End of the Trail* statue, we had several of the pictures at home, she found one in a shop, and I bought it for her not realizing what a poor choice it was. I knew it would be our last anniversary, that kind of love was dead, incredibly sad, just when things could not get worse at home, they did. We began to fight on an everyday basis. Now it was mean; and we had no qualms about throwing something or breaking something, even picking up a could be weapon in a threatening manner. I locked up the guns. By mid fall I decided we had to separate. I could go, or she could go. If not, this would end in prison time for the one who survived. I told her she could stay and pay her own bills, and I would be gone, or she could go anywhere, just be gone. I would support her until she got sober and back on her feet.

She left and went to her sister's, mainly because without my income, she could not do anything. I was relieved. We had no plan for divorce, just peace. After a week, her sister was done and asked her to leave. She wanted to come home, but I told her not until she was sober, and then I had the locks changed. I did not trust her family for sure. Her rage was scary. I was certain that if she could get certain family members to help, I would come home to an empty house or worse.

The entire family was outraged with me, and I am certain this was a really wrong thing to do. I cannot imagine how this all looked to the people looking on. No one had an alternate solution, so I went with mine. I rented an apartment, furnished it, provided all her needs. I supervised while she came and got her stuff, not helped, supervised. I offered and even insisted we get help. For the first time, I suggested couples help and joint alcohol treatment. Her family screamed at me but offered no sanctuary for her at their homes or financial help to help get her treatment.

It was ugly on all fronts. We could not even be in the same room without a fight starting, so treatment did not get scheduled. She stayed at the apartment, and she called when the bills needed paid. I paid them. She applied for disability, telling me she had really given up on herself, me, marriage, and life in general. We were separated in every sense of the word. It was a terrible winter; holidays were just a time to cry and drink, and communication stopped. Her family had been my family for twenty-five years, and it was gone, all gone.

Valentine's Day came and went, and I hid from my birthday in March as much as possible. The road to the cabin opened in late April, and I did not care. I made a solo trip or two to check on it but never opened it for use. The love for the cabin was dead also; it was no longer a happy place. It just did not matter. I was as sick as could be and down thirty-five pounds, and my balance was off, so I fell a lot. The high altitude in Winfield was brutal.

I had no idea how Glenna was doing; my addiction was all I cared about. It is amazing I still went to work every day and earned a living. Hindsight tells me my business associates were sick of my antics and were only hanging in there with me out of respect and the small hope that I would eventually recover. Her birthday in May 2016 would be the big 6-0. We spoke about it; she wanted to go to the cabin. I did not or could not, and I knew full well it would be impossible together. In a drunken moment, I told her to use her old key and "go alone like I do." I knew she could not and would not. I threw her a bone and offered a nice dinner. That was a "No" and her unrelenting phone calls and foul mouth made me just withdraw. It was horrible; I was no help. This person, who had been my best friend, my lover, my hunting buddy, my wife, my everything, the one I would grow old with, was now my archenemy. I had no clue on what to do, so I did nothing.

Her birthday passed; I did not even call her. Pathetic.

June arrived with no fanfare, just more of the same at home. I needed a break, so I headed for the cabin, partly to show her that I could do what I wanted when I wanted to. I was still in charge. I had not spoken with Glenna since the birthday episode and had no idea how things were in her world. I rolled without telling anyone I was going or when I would be back. I had to go within a few miles of one of her family members, one who was particularly upset about the whole thing. I was feeling sorry for myself, but it got worse when I pulled into the driveway and knocked on the door. After some repeated criticism, I insisted we talked about what to do for Glenna. They had seen her that day and tried to take her to the hospital because she was turning yellow, but she would not go. Things got heated; I left and headed west.

When I arrived at the cabin, it finally had eaten me alive. I never unlocked the door; I got back in the truck and went home. The next day I was at her apartment door early. I had to make a loud ruckus to get a response from inside. I could tell by her voice she was drunk. I threatened to break the door down if she failed to open it, so she did.

She was incredibly thin, yellow, shaking, scared, and mad. I started to call 911, but she said she would go. We headed to the

ER again. She was admitted and evaluated. She was shutting down. Her liver, kidneys, pancreas, her heart rate, respiration, temperature were all out of normal ranges. Asking if she would make it was nearly impossible; the words would not form. "It is up to her" was the prognosis.

She was coherent enough to know I was there. I held her hand and told her I loved her, but all she could do was a weak squeeze. She pulled down the oxygen mask covering her face and so softly said, "You don't need to come back tomorrow".

I'll be back I said, squeezing her hand as she faded away. I was back early the next day, but when I walked into her room she was gone; they had taken her to ICU. There, the doctors put her into a coma to rest her body. Six days passed without a word from her lips. On the seventh day in a meeting with her doctors, they informed me she was brain dead. The next day I made the hard decision and held her hand while she died. It was the end of her trail. I have a lot more to say about this, but I will keep it where it is for now.

The end of her trail.

The first few days were nothing, no thoughts, no memory, just numbness. Just empty, I went through the motions of the right thing to do. She was a donor, so I signed that paperwork. I called the funeral home so her body could be picked up afterward and cremated according to her wishes. She wanted to be at the big headstone in the Winfield Cemetery with her brother Denis, Too Tall Brother we called him, who we had spread there a decade before.

Services were planned and executed according to her wishes. Her family wanted her services elsewhere; I gave them part of her ashes so they could have their own separate service. I was asked to not attend theirs, and only a few family members came to Winfield for the one I planned. I remember the day in a dream kind of way. My daughter Chelsea drove me there. I had to drink just to deal with the day.

We all walked up to the place near the headstone, and Uncle Rodger said some words about her life and how she loved the mountains and how she loved life and how she loved me. I remember thinking how true those words once were and that most gathered there had no idea how the last few years had been for her and me. I spread the first hand full of her ashes, then those who chose to stepped forward and did the same. No more pain. Revelation 21:4 says, "*And God shall wipe away all tears from their eyes; and there shall be no more death, neither sorrow, nor crying, neither shall there be any more pain: for the former things are passed away.*"

Now I was angry. How could God allow this terrible thing to happen? She had made a deal with Him, and because he was a forgiving God, why was she not forgiven of her failure to keep her end of the bargain and stop drinking? Now I was alone. This was not fair; how could she do this to me after all the wonderful things I had done for her? Poor me, poor me, pour me another drink. I most certainly was not to blame for her death like Doctor O. said I would be. I gave her every chance to not drink my liquor. It was his fault; he was the doctor not me. I never forced a drink down her throat. She snuck it, even after I put her through rehab twice. What if *I'da* done things differently?

She cannot really be gone; this is a dream. I will wake up, go home, and she will be sitting in her spot on the sofa with her nice comfy pajamas on, with a twinkle in her eye, sober, with dinner on the table. We would have dinner with a nice glass of wine. It would be like we had planned it, we would grow old together, defying the odds and living to be 100. But reality said otherwise. I needed to figure out how not to die.

No cabin, no flag, no Charlie, no anniversary, no memory of the next two months. Going through the motions of life became life, the shock of it all slowly soaking in. The calls from family and what friends were left stopped coming. I am sure my daily appearances at the office were unproductive and mostly frustrating for my associates. I had received the pay out on her life insurance by now, so I was not in need of cash, a bad thing, I think. It allowed me to skip any meaningful sleep, have a drink or two to take the edge off, show up at work, pretend I was a Realtor for a while, and then go home and drink the rest of the day away in my misery.

The relentless cycle continued into October until one day while at home in the middle of the afternoon indulging in my addiction alone, the doorbell rang. I stumbled over there to chew out who ever it happened to be took a minute and it rang again. A very grouchy, what do you want? rolled out of my mouth as the door opened. Wow! I was surprised at first; it was a group of my friends from work. How nice, but in a few seconds, it hit me.

I only had one friend left, and they were here to take it away. This was not just a friendly visit. They insisted I go with them to the CDU and let them check me in, *NOW*, to get me some help. It sounded all too familiar, and I was *out*! I defiantly sat there with drink in hand and informed them that I am in charge and doing just fine.

They persisted, I wondered just how mean and nasty I would need to get to make them leave? My disposition quickly turned to; you can't make me. I am an adult and of sound mind and body. Back and forth for a while it went, each of them taking a turn at me. Expressing their sorrow and concern, they finally left. How stupid do I look to them I wondered? None of the things I just said were true, and I knew it. I do not remember who all was there that day, but if you were and you are reading this, I thank you. A seed had been planted; my life had been saved.

After the night got to the long, quiet part, more like early morning, I prayed to a God I did not know or understand to help me. It was the first time I ever *needed* Him. A moment of clarity came to me, though I did not recognize it then; it was an answered prayer. I resolved that I would quit, now it boiled down to when? No idea how, that would need to come. It would be a long haul; most likely I would need to be out of the loop for a time. The biggest loose end was the cabin; it was still open and would need to be closed for the winter while I got sober. I could not go there again with all Glenna's stuff still there. I asked Karen, my business partner, and her husband Robert to go with me the next weekend and be the clean-out crew. They knew Glenna well; it would be hard, but she agreed. They would be doing me huge favor.

Chapter 6
SEEKING GOD

IT WAS FALL, THE TIME WE WOULD HAVE been hunting; cool days and colder nights were upon us. Snow would fly soon, closing the road once again. The mountains were gorgeous, still deep green with bits of new gold below timberline, holding on to the final bits of summer, with cold rock above and light snow on the peaks. A faint elk bugled now and then far up the valley.

Normally, this was my favorite time. Our arrival in Winfield was somber as we knew what we would do in the next twenty-four hours. It would be hard. We had all been friends for twenty-five years, a foursome. Robert's cabin name was Stud Muffin, Karen was Big Red, Glenna was Wilderness Woman, and I was Winfield Willy. Now there were three. The day was young, so we dug right in. Starting with the coat rack next to the front door, things were removed, shown to me for judgment, then put back where they were or bagged in the toss bag or the donate bag and then out to Robert's waiting truck. One thing at a time, she was being removed from our lives. There were tears, many pauses to remember a good time, then more tears.

Cabin cleanout day and Winfield Peak where the flag goes.

It was mostly just hard. The sadness would not leave me. Although I had made plans to stop drinking, I rationalized that this was not the time to start the process. We all had a few, I had more than I should have. Then to the closet, then to the dresser, shoes, my goodness the woman had shoes. Slippers, boots, hiking shoes, water shoes, hats, gloves, glasses, magazines, I finally said take them all and donate them. Sheets, pillows, towels, make up, brushes, medications, it all had to go. By evening, the job was mostly done. I shared the story of Charlie Jones with my good friends. I asked for help; what does it mean? Is there a message in there that I do not or cannot see? The long day and the drinks took over before any discussion took place. Karen and Robert retired to the master bedroom. I had not slept there for a long time, so they might as well enjoy the comfort. I stayed up, no sleep.

The next morning, as I lifted my head from my crossed arms in the same spot where I had been the night before, I saw it was still very dark outside. I needed to be quiet, but my guests would want hot coffee soon, and it would not make itself, so after waiting a while to be sure and to regain a clear head,

I made a pot. The coffee cooked a bit and began to perk. It smelled good. A long time has passed since my last cup. Better to drink coffee than whisky for breakfast, even if it made me sick. What a concept, hot coffee first thing in the morning. If I could start there and make a huge effort, could I not drink today? Probably not, but let's try.

Coffee in hand, I sat back down. The candlelight got help from the now-rising sun so I could see the puzzle pieces from the storytelling the night before on the table. The rings, the stick, the headstone picture all on the open map. The nail and the twenty were on the wood tabletop closer to me. They were separated, the bill was sort of flattened out from us looking at the "too much" cut marks. The nail was on top of it. The twenty belonged on the nail, when I touched it, it almost folded automatically after over two years of fold memory, placing it back on the nail was easy now, then I just dropped it on the table in front of me. Looking down at the rejoined pieces brought tears to my eyes. I am sure my heart stopped at what I saw. On the top side of the fold, I could see the word GOD showing as plain as day, it had been there from the beginning, only I could not see it, I wasn't *Paying Attention*. I now had a big part of the meaning of the rusty spike through the *Bill* • It was Jesus Christ in me, God through my heart, the mystery, sobbing uncontrollably, I woke my guests by accident. Karen, who is saved, came out first.

The moment I knew I need God and I needed to Pay Attention.

"What is wrong?" I showed her, and we had a moment. Then she nailed it: "*God* is talking to you, Bill. *"Pay Attention"* for your own sake. There it is in writing. What else do you want?" were her words. I wanted Him from that moment on, I did not know what it was or how to get it, but I wanted it absolutely. I needed someone to show me. The Ethiopian story was a clue. It is found in Acts 8:31 saying, *"And he said, How can I except some man should show me. And he desired Philip that he would come up and sit with him."* I was seeking God.

We were all emotionally exhausted so the winterization would have to wait for one more week, Now I could do that myself in one more trip, soon. Would Charlie be here? My attitude had made a big adjustment in the right direction, and I was certain I could stop drinking. I was still missing the how, but I was *Paying Attention*, and I would know it when I saw it. The need to drink was still with me but on short notice this time.

November arrived sooner than it should have. A big snowstorm was predicted for the fifteenth, no doubt the one that would close the road for the year. I had to get things up the mountain winterized. The need to drink was not an emotional need but simply a requirement to keep my body from shutting down, I think. I was using it more like medicine in metered amounts but still more than I should; sobriety was weak in me. I read everything I could on the proper way to stop, check in, get help, come off slow or it could kill you was the message. Not sure I could do it that way. The twelfth was the magic date. I could go and get the chores done, lock it up, then see it again next spring... sober, I prayed.

Up the mountain I went, feeling somewhat victorious simply because I felt like I had a tiny bit of power over my addiction. I did not drink on the way there; it was a miracle. In no time at all, the water was drained, the wood was stocked, the fridge was shut down, mouse traps put out, and all the preparations for bitter cold had been made. I made an evening trip to the cemetery just in case Charlie was hanging around. It was strange to walk there sober. I sat on the headstone where Glenna and Dennis were resting. Sitting with them, I asked God to confirm that He was real that He was there with me. I begged for a sign. I tried to *Pay Attention*, but nothing happened. I yelled it, louder, *SHOW ME!* I waited until dark. Nothing.

The next day would be mine to look for Charlie and make more peace with my addiction. I spent the evening with great anticipation. Sleep escaped me, still waiting for something to happen. Looking at the clock, I saw it was 1:00 a.m. It was faint, but it was there, a sign. This time of year, the aspen trees are bare, the leaves of summer have fallen to the ground to complete the cycle of life, and the water they once held has fallen back down the core into the roots. They are dry and hardened, ready for the cold. It is a rare thing and one of my favorites, one of those that had always given me a chill and a deep appreciation of God's creation. When the wind would blow down the valley, exactly right, the tops of the aspens would knock together.

It was as though Sherwood Forest was reborn. The sound is a phenomenon, countless treetops playing an orchestra in perfect timing with the gentle gusts. Only twice had this happened in all my fall visits to God's country. It had to be a sign, and as I jumped up and rushed to the kitchen window for a look, I saw it. The harvest moon was huge in the sky and as bright as day. This was one of Glenna's favorite things. It had to be a sign. The words of Charlie Jones ran through my memory. "I roam from ancient cemetery to ancient cemetery; you *will* be surprised what you *can* find there, *if you Pay Attention.*" I needed to go. I felt as though a friend was there with me, a friend who was in charge, I wanted to be guided. He wanted me to guide me in return. Boots on, up the road to the cemetery at 2:00 a.m., I was alone? Was I really?

top; the harvest moon from the cemetery. Bottom; the walk up to the rock.

It was an easy walk; nature's band played on and lit my way straight to the big stone where I had been asking for a sign not long ago. I sat down. The view was incredible, and the trees played on. I cried out; *God help me. Come to me.* The music stopped; it became still, and at that moment a power greater than I had ever felt engulfed me.

It was love, it was reassurance, it was safety; it told me I would be okay, no matter what. I cried. I believe the Holy Spirit was there, and a door had been opened to me at that moment. I did not know what had happened, but I liked it; it was a good thing. I sat for a long time until the sun came up.

Winfield Cemetery. The headstone in the back slight right of center marks Glenna and Dennis's resting place. This is where God came to me that night and everything changed.

Heading back down, I was a totally different man, and I had to find out what had happened. I did not know what it was, but the old man was gone, and a new man was in his place. I think the mail had been delivered. Now it was up to me to open it.

Back home, I expected something, not sure what, but something. Had I been saved? Was all this the reason for Charlie's visit? Why did I still want to drink? Life was the same other than my awareness that something had happened. I was unaware of God's ways, and I did not know that I needed to "come to him" rather than wait for him to come to me. The visit at the cemetery was but a short glimpse of the mystery.

Thanksgiving was brutal, even though I got invitations from family, friends, and even strangers. I didn't want to be with anyone; I couldn't celebrate. Thankful for what? Instead I ran. My frail sobriety collapsed. I would need to find this God fellow later, if I made it to later. Into the dented truck, jug of Crown Royal in hand, I drove. I am not sure where I ended up, but I logged 1,000 miles on Thanksgiving Day before returning home on Friday only long enough to realize I could not be there, either. I had my .45 ACP in the truck, like I always did. I went to the ammo cabinet and selected *the bullet*, just in case I did not want to do this anymore, rationalizing it would be the easier road.

Another jug, another journey, another 1,000 miles on Friday. I do not remember getting home, but I know it was Saturday very early. I slept it off, clothes on, face down, on the floor. When I came to, the bullet had worked its way from my pocket and was staring me in the face; it was decision time. Life or death? It was my choice, and I had to make it. A little flash of the feeling I had on the rock ran through me. I wanted to live. I stopped.

By Monday, withdrawal had me in its grip, I don't remember, but I am told that Manda, one of my team, drove me to the ER where I was admitted and taken to the main hospital. I was sober, nearly dead, but I was sober. I was headed to rehab. The stay is a blur. I remember bits and pieces. I do know that somehow the gift given me during that moment at the cemetery was still in there and was now giving me strength. Now that my addiction was not blocking the ability to *Pay Attention*, I now sat about the business of seeking God.

My life depended on my finding him. I had so much to discover, so much to learn. The first thing I learned is that God does not yell; He simply whispers. I could hear him if I chose to. How, was still my question. Who is He, where is He, and why is He? In lockup, we were required to attend classes. They told me I should admit I had a problem and that I was beaten, powerless over alcohol. That was easy; all one needed to do was go try the locked door. I was powerless alright; it had ruined my life, and I not only let it, I helped it.

Next, I had to admit I needed help and not from rehab but a power greater than me and greater than them. I made the connection to the power I felt on the rock. It was the power I needed; I was sure of it. Then, I would need to turn my will over to this power as I understood it. I didn't understand anything about it, if it was in fact God. I was on the right path for the first time in my life.

It was early December, I was out of lock up, I was sober and at my task of seeking God. My doctor from the rehab center decided I was depressed and prescribed something to help me stay sober and steady. I took one, headed for home and had a DUI in less than an hour. Now I was depressed. I drank and drove for decades and never got stopped, but now I was sober, not one drop of alcohol on board, just prescription drugs taken as prescribed. I guess God thought I needed it. It was just another steppingstone in my journey.

The court ordered me to attend classes and self-help groups with other alcoholics who were looking for a better way to live. I believe this was God working in my life. What one man can do, another man can do, so follow a leader. In one particular group, the people who seemed to have it together also seemed to know about God. Each one explained that God was there and available, but none really had a road map. They said God would do for me what I could not do for myself if I sought Him, but it would take time. How would I find him? I surmised that seeking Him would be good enough for now and that when the time came, I would know. Just stay sober one day at a time, keep being around sober people, and seek God. This was my plan.

Each day brought more clarity, more energy, and more desire to gain understanding of the God spoken about in my groups. It never dawned on me that a church would be a good place to start, even though a good friend of mine, Cheryl, who worked at one of the title companies kept inviting me to go to hers but not in a pushy, holier than thou kind of way. More like in a genuine way, just as a friend, she could probably see I needed to be there. I respectfully declined her invitation several times, mostly out of fear I suspect. We saw each other regularly in business and had conversations but not always about church, mostly about life. She knew a little about the recent tragedy in my life, so I was not totally surprised when she mentioned Sheila, a friend of hers.

It seemed Sheila was also single and liked many of the same things I did, like the great outdoors, fishing, hunting, and hiking. Cheryl gave me her number to call. The idea was we could be friends, maybe more down the road. I was scared to death and didn't call, not right away. I had no plan to call her for any reason. Then a few days later, seeing her number lying next to the phone at home, Charlie's words ran through my head, Pay Attention. Wondering if this was something, I should Pay Attention to, I called, but her voice mail answered. My message had to be less than encouraging, who I was, where I got her number, and don't bother to call back.

It wasn't long and she called me back. The time passed quickly, and we connected. I knew she was a Christian because she told me so. I could tell she had what I wanted: she understood God. A few conversations later, we made plans to meet face to face, eat a sandwich down by the reservoir, and enjoy the sunset. The dinner and scenery were a bust, cold and cloudy, and she did not like sandwiches, but the conversation afterward was pay dirt. We sat and talked; I could see in her eyes that she had something I wanted. I did not know for sure, but I was thinking it was the mystery I had been seeking, it was God.

I told her bits and pieces of my story, trying not to make her think I was crazy, but it was not making any sense. I came clean, thinking I would never see her again, but I told this whole story. She listened intently, and when I got to the part about seeing in her what I wanted.

"I know a man you need to talk to" was her response. "His name is Pastor Bigler. Will you go to church with me?" was the question.

Yes, was my immediate answer. The following Sunday, we attended together. The words spoken in the sermon rang true; I needed to find Jesus Christ and accept him as my Savior. I wanted to find him, and this man knew the way. Finally, a clear path. Pastor Bigler and I made plans to meet twice a week, starting that Tuesday. I had to know more. I attended church with Sheila on Wednesdays and Sundays, and she helped me to understand more as we went. The message was loud and clear, and on February 22, 2017, I understood Him enough to turn my life over to Jesus Christ, my God, and He saved me. The Holy Spirit entered me and took a solid hold. I was saved, *AMEN!* I was baptized at Heritage Baptist Church on February 23, 2017.

Chapter 7
EVIDENCE LIST

LOOKING BACK AND TRYING TO THINK in a in a logical way, I asked myself, Is there a God? What evidence of this can I see as a man just seeking something better? I could see this world was not random in its creation; for one, there is just no possible way it fell together. Nothing falls together. Have you ever planted a garden? Look how much work must be done to make it grow. It must be the time of year to grow a garden to begin with, then the ground must be prepared, proper seed selected and planted properly, then it must be watered and weeded in order to get just one little plant to grow and produce fruit. How does your garden grow if you miss just one step? Poorly or not at all.

Then compare the forests of the entire world to your one small patch, really, random? Try building a house by first making all the material somehow, then throw it in a pile and wait. A house will not build itself, no matter how long you wait. It will not evolve no matter how long you wait; it simply will not. It's not random. How about the design of us? Mankind has been trying since the days of Adam and Eve to figure out how we work, all the intricate systems, all built in, working with and relying on one another.

Why does our heartbeat? Why does our blood coagulate? How do we think? How does pain and discomfort work? Why do you like red and I like blue? You like hot and I like cold? I am up early, and you sleep late. The ones that no science can explain for sure are love and hate. It is endless. It is because we are all made by God, all different, unique individuals.

Imagine, the same God that made the world, the oceans and the deserts and the mountains, the plants, animals, water and air also made you. You are handmade, one of a kind. What other possible answer is there? There isn't. Now, I know science says it has the answers to some of these questions but really? They analyze the how down to neurons and protons, God made those as well. Science can look for the how but the why was explained to me in the first book of the Bible, in Genesis 1:1 says, *"In the Beginning God Created the heaven and the earth."*

Then in the next six days, literal days, He created all we see around us. He created light and dark, then dry land and water, then the plants and cycles of day and night, then seasons, days and years, then the sun and the moon, then the creatures of the water and the winged foul of the air, then the animals and insects. So, think about it, the stage was set; it was ready for mankind to be created. Then on the sixth day God said, "Let us make man in our image, after our likeness." I think the "us" is Father God, Jesus Christ, and the Holy Spirit. He created man, but before He did, He gave us dominion over all He had just created.

John 1:3 says, *"All things were made by him; and without him was not any thing made that was made."* I love this because it is so plain, it says *"All things"* not, a few things or some things, *"All things."* It is simple really. Either God is, or God is not. The evidence is so overwhelming that God is, it did not take me long to come to understand the why. The why is because we were in fact created by God; He made us, and we need Him.

He designed us in His image. This is the way of life. We will believe things we see on TV, on the web, even on Facebook as fact, truth, just because it is there. Think about this: The Bible *is* the Word of God. I believe, the truth, the light, the way. Do you not need to know more about it? I do.

BIBLE:
Basic
Instructions
Before
Leaving
Earth.

Each person has their own story about how they were saved by Jesus Christ; you have just read mine. I admit mine seems hard to believe, and you may think I am completely out of my mind. You also know that at one time I was overly concerned with what other people would think if I shared my testimony with them. I am no longer concerned about that, as I now live my life in a way that I am certain God is pleased with me, and that is the only thing I am concerned with. I can say this, knowing I am far from perfect but that the love God has for me is unconditional.

When I was saved, I knew enough to be certain I was ready to let go of control of my life and turn it over to the only one who could make a difference in how the rest of my life would go. I did not have any biblical knowledge, no training in spiritual things, no special skills, nothing that all of us don't have in us, including you. The words Pastor Bigler spoke rang true as we began to study God's Word. He made sure the things I learned were God's word, not his. The first thing he read was from John 1:1, it says, "*In the beginning was the Word, and the Word was with God, and the Word Was God.*" Now, considering I am a simple man and take things quite literally, this told me that the Bible is the Word of God and that Christ is the Word of God. They are not only related, but they are also the same. It made sense to me that because I wanted to know and understand more about the Word of God, this is where I should look. Now, I know that the Bible is the handbook to life, and any problem you may be facing the answer is in this book. All one needs to do is open your heart and seek it out. So, I got started. I pray you do too.

On February 20, 2017, I bought my first very own King James Version Bible. Pastor Bigler told me this was the purest and most accurate Bible available, and it was important that I learned the correct way. I began to read and explore the Word of God. God made us in his own image, and in doing so, He also gave us free will. He started us in the Garden of Eden; I can't imagine what that was like. It was a perfect place for us. He made Adam, then Eve. The free will is where the problems started.

He gave a simple set of instructions for them to follow in the garden. Adam was to dress and keep the garden, and they could eat from any tree except one, the tree of knowledge of good and evil. That was forbidden. We all know the story of how the serpent (Satan) tempted Eve, she submitted to temptation, then convinced Adam it was a good idea, and they both disobeyed God and ate the forbidden fruit. This created sin. Adam and Eve felt guilt and shame for the first time; they knew what they had done was wrong and hid from God. He found them and cursed the garden.

God punished man with hard work and toil, the woman was punished with the pain of childbirth, and the serpent was to crawl in the dust forever and eventually will be destroyed.

God drove Adam and Eve from the garden and declared someone would be born of a woman someday, who would do battle with the serpent and win. From that moment on, sin and guilt from sin has been man's problem. Sin became so bad in only a few generations that God cleansed the world with a great flood. It is another Bible story we are all familiar with, now consider, this happened, and we see proof of it here and now.

God loves us unconditionally, He does, however, have rules that are spelled out in the Bible. The Old Testament tells of how God's chosen people committed sins against God, then were forgiven and saved (and many times chastised by God), and then committed more sin against God. Pastor and I went over the Ten Commandments in Exodus 20. (Full text printed in scripture readings at the back of the book.) These are the words of God, spoken to Moses. If a person could and would follow all these perfectly, heart, mind, and soul, he could be sin free. We cannot do this because God also gave us free will. Throughout the Old Testament, when God's rules were followed, blessings also were bestowed as God promised. It is an amazing history of how and why we are where we are.

At the end of the Old Testament, the stage is set for the chosen one to come to us here on Earth, fully human and fully God. The last book, Malachi, makes a prediction. Malachi 3-1 says, *"Behold, I will send my messenger, and he shall prepare the way before me: and the LORD, whom ye seek, shall suddenly come to his temple, even the messenger of the covenant, whom you delight in: behold he shall come, saith the LORD of hosts."* After this prophecy was made, 400 years passed until God spoke directly to man, and the New Testament began.

The New Testament is the story of Jesus Christ and how he was sent to Earth to spread the word of God, live a perfect life free from sin, and die on the cross for all our sins. It is not about religion; it is about a person having a spiritual connection with God through Jesus Christ. Religion is one of any number of manmade rituals and teaching concepts. Religion is criticized many times in the Bible by Christ Himself. In Matthew 23, verses 13, 14, 15, 16, 23, 25, 27 and 29-30 all begin with, *"Woe to you, scribes and Pharisees, hypocrites!"* (Full text printed in scripture readings at the back of the book.)

This is about salvation, not the Old Testament kind like when God swooped in and saved Moses or David. I believe God can and does save us like He did them many times without us even realizing it. When you think about it and *Pay Attention*, I am certain you can recall a time in your own life when God saved you from disaster without question; there is evidence to prove it. I believe when we are saved, God is involved in the details of our lives, He knows us. It is about salvation, right-now salvation, the kind that sets us free from pride, greed, lust, envy, gluttony, wrath, sloth, guilt, worry, anger, and frustration, and allows us to live our daily lives in love. John 3:16 says, *"For God so loved the world, that he gave his only begotten Son, that whosoever believeth in him should not perish, but have everlasting life."* Salvation is God's way to forgive sin and provide a means for man to receive eternal life now and in heaven.

The very second anyone accepts Jesus Christ as his personal Lord and Savior and believes in his heart in Jesus, he will receive eternal life. The old sinful spirit dies and the Holy Spirit will indwell the new Christian. We show this to God by confessing our sins and turning genuinely from our sinful ways to God's ways. It is that simple; it cannot be gained by works or by tithing or by any other means. It is simply a gift from God by His grace through Jesus Christ who died on the cross that all sins are forgiven. This is the only way to become saved. Jesus said so. John 14:6 says, *"I am the way, the truth, and the life: no man cometh unto the Father, but by me."* The Bible has many such verses, making it clear Jesus is the only way to make the connection with God. The good news is this can be done anywhere, anytime.

God is omnipresent; He is right here with me right now, and at this very moment, He is there with you right now. I have made the choice to hear Him, feel Him, and accept Him. I know He is here with me. Do you know He is there with you? If not, you can. The Bible also tells us that He is always listening, God hears all prayers and answers everyone. His answer may be no, yes, not now, or I have something better in mind.

The prayers of a sinner are heard to be sure; He does not answer them unless you have faith. Matthew 21:22 says, *"And all things, whatever ye shall ask in prayer, believing, ye shall receive."* He only answers prayer through our faith in Jesus Christ. He wants us all to be saved and wants to hear our prayers.

> Jeremiah 29:12-13 says, *"Then shall ye call upon me, and ye shall go and pray unto me, and I will hearken unto you. And ye shall seek me, and find me, when ye shall search for me with your heart."*

> 1 John 5:14-15 says, *"And this is the confidence that we have in him, that, if we ask anything according to his will, He heareth us: And if we know He hear us, whatsoever we ask, we know we have the petitions we desire of him."*

> Matthew 7:7 says, *"Ask and ye shall find; knock and it shall be opened to you."*

If you are like I was and thought it was enough to just believe there was a God, sort of, you pray like I did. When in trouble, or ready to cut a deal with God to get what you want, then you will need to work on it a bit. The first key is to believe in Jesus Christ as your Savior and have faith in him, turning your life over to him. We are shown how in Acts 8:31. When the Ethiopian did not understand the reading, he said to Philip, *"How can I except some man should guide me? And he desired Philip that he would come up and sit with him."* Your guide can be anyone: a pastor, a friend, or a relative, plus reading and study of the Bible. Sometimes faith comes slowly, sometimes quickly, but it will *always* happen if it is sought.

I can only speak for me and my experience as a baby Christian, knowing you will be in a different place in life than I was when it happened to me. You may be way worse off; your sins may be eating you alive from the inside out like mine were. You may still be as I was, in charge, and not ready to receive the gift of salvation and release all that pain. Your story will be different, faster, I hope. It took me fifty-six years to figure it out. It may be that yours will be slower; I do not know. I do know that Jesus has removed from me the desire to drink, and had this not happened, I would be dead. I believe God has always been there and available to me; all I needed to do was accept Jesus into my heart and all my sin would have been forgiven, and it has now.

You may think your sins are too evil, and there is no way these will be forgiven; this is wrong. Sin is sin; God sees and knows about all sin. This is why He sent Jesus to die on the cross and make atonement for *all* sin, large or small. In your heart and mind, they will all be forgiven when you accept Jesus; He paid for our sins in full on the cross. Another thing I believed was that now that I am saved, I had to be perfect in

God's eyes or face His wrath. This is not true; once saved we are forgiven forever. There are many verses in the Bible that speak of this. John 10:28 says,

> *"And I give unto them eternal life; and they shall never parish, neither shall any man pluck them out of my hands. John 3:16, For God so loved the world, that he gave his only begotten Son, that whosoever shall believeth in Him, shall not perish, but have everlasting life."*

Again, it is quite simple, the Bible says forever, so it is forever. Anyone who tells you salvation can be lost is wrong. It is possible to fall away from God as described in some verses, but this would mean true salvation was never there in the heart; it was the faith that was missing. First John 2:4 says, *"He that saith, I know Him, and keepeth not his commandments, is a liar, and the truth is not in him."* The Bible states clearly that God does not remember our sin. Hebrews 8:12 says, *"For I will be merciful to their unrighteousness, and their sins and iniquities will I remember no more."* This is just one verse; this promise is repeated in several other places throughout God's Word.

I only wish I could forgive this way and simply forget it. We all sin every day, we are human, and God knows this. He wants our actions and intension to be a life of Christ. He knows we will make mistakes; He wants us to be seeking him. Once we are saved and the Holy Spirit is in us, it is easy to know right from wrong. When tempted by sin or confused, we need only to ask for guidance, and it will be given to us through prayer. Progress not perfection.

All of this is on my evidence list to be certain. The world around us was created by God. There is no possible way it just grew from sea foam or evolved all on its own by chance. I can see a horse run, watch a child cry, and feel the wind blow and know this for certain. Knowing I was created by God and have been given the gift of salvation is also on my list. It is a beautiful thing to know it is there for the taking; all we need to do is ask for it and accept it and believe it, and it shall be given. Amen!

Chapter 8
POUR IT OUT, POUR IT IN, POUR IT OUT

MY DAILY HABIT BECAME READING THE Bible. I read it cover to cover in a few days less than six months. I could not get enough of the Word of God.

> Matthew 22:37-40 says, *"Thou shalt love the Lord thy God with all thy heart, and with all thy soul, and with all thy mind. This is the first and great commandment. And the second is like unto it, Thou shalt love thy neighbor as thy self. On these two commandments hang all the law and the prophets."*

It intrigued me; this was the opposite of the way the old me thought, back then it was all about me. I had much to learn. Pastor Bigler and I continued our weekly fellowship meetings, only now they had a new twist. Sheila Joe and I had decided we would marry, so the studies became premarital counseling, biblical teachings of how a couple should conduct themselves during the courting time, up to and including the big day and afterward. We agreed we would plan our wedding, study hard, and observe biblical principles, no matter what. We would be setting the example for our children and grandchildren. Sheila Joe already knew and understood this plan, but I had to learn it.

I wanted to do this right; not like I had done it in the past. Part of what I learned as I started to understand how I needed to conduct my new life was that I knew things needed to change, and now I was seeking the how. As I spent time with Pastor, he began to point out messages in the Bible known as parables. These were short stories used by Jesus to make a point, to teach a biblical principal of living intermingled in various books of the Bible. These are not biblical fables as some suggest; these are metaphors that tell us how we should live life, not in a direct way but in a way that if the one being told does not know Jesus in his heart, the words would just sound like gibberish. The messages given were always just a little ambiguous, the meaning for the listener to be determined by the listener to some extent. These are the truth, they were then, they are now and will be forever, applicable throughout the ages.

I needed to *Pay Attention* and really concentrate on how these words could and would apply to me, to my way of thinking, my new way of life. These parables spoke to me, the mystery within them started to make me want to change, to apply these to my life in a way that it made sense to me. This took me way back to when I started to want to find God. The revelation came to me that this is what was meant when I was told to turn my life and my will over to God "as I understood him • This *was* understanding Him. I got it! I could understand Him, with faith, belief, time with the Word of God, prayer for understanding and *Paying Attention.*

The first parable that soaked into this degree is in Matthew 9:16, it says, *"No man putteth a piece of new cloth unto an old garment, for that which is put in to fill it up taketh from the garment, and the rent is made worse."* Think about it. In those days any garment worn by the average Joe was old and worn from the way it existed. So, should you get a tear in it and if you patched it with new cloth, when the new cloth shrank, it would ruin the repair and ruin the entire garment, not something any one would do that had a tiny bit of common sense. This would have meant nothing to the old me. I would have scratched my head to think it means anything at all.

Now, to me this meaning was clear. My old self was the old garment worn out from sin; from the way I had lived my life up until the day I was saved. The lesson here is that I needed to not to patch my old spirit with the new spirit that was now in me. I had to put my old ways aside completely, repent of my sins, and begin to live the way God's Word guides me. The scripture tells me in 2 Corinthians 5:17, saying I am made new: *"Therefore if any man be in Christ, he is a new creature: old things are passed away; behold, all things are become new."* Now I could let God be in charge and guide my thoughts and my actions. What a relief to be not in charge, to let God's Word guide me through life.

The second parable that really made sense to me sparked a change as well. This one found in Matthew 9:1 says, *"Neither do men put new wine into old bottles: else the bottles break, and the wine runneth out, and the bottles perish: but they put new wine into new bottles, and both are preserved."* This parable tells me much the same thing as the first. If a new spiritual connection is to survive, it cannot be put in an old container. The container being my soul, my heart, the old me, must be changed to new. Out with the old and in with new, as Mom always said. Both Mom and the Bible told me I must change the way I went about life, new thoughts, new habits, new love for God and everyone around me.

This would be hard. It was, it is, and it will be moving forward. It may be hard, but it is something I want to do. Luke 16:10 says, *"He that is faithful in that which is least is faithful also in much: and he that is unjust in the least is unjust also in much."* This verse tells me I must start to be faithful in the small things, and when I follow Jesus, it will become my nature to act as a Christian in all things, large and small.

Along about this time, Sheila Joe and I were beginning to form a strong bond with Pastor Bigler and his lovely wife Jan. Not only were we friends but part of the same church family, and Pastor was our spiritual leader. Sheila had been encouraging to me to share my testimony with them, but I was afraid Pastor would not believe me or ask questions that I did not have answers for. His biblical knowledge was immense, and mine was nonexistent. I was afraid I would look like an idiot in front of them, and they would find this whole thing unbelievable. With Sheila Joe's assurance that because it was *my* testimony and it happened the way it happened, I should be proud of it and share it with anyone who would listen. After all, no one can argue with anyone's personal testimony; it is the tellers to tell.

Of course, at the time, she knew way more about pouring it out than I did. She knew the calling of the Word of God is to share the Good News. So, I agreed to share it with the Pastor and Jan, and a time and date was set. When they arrived at our home for dinner, I was off the chart nervous but determined to tell it like it happened and to stand behind my testimony no matter what their reaction was. As the words came out, the reaction from them both was one of intense interest and deep emotion. There were some tears and looks of amazement as I told the story.

Nearly as soon as I was done Pastor suggested I write it down, get it recorded, do a slide show, even share it in church, something to enable more people to experience it as a powerful tool to spread the Good News. This was the first time I shared my testimony with anyone who I thought would have a probability of disputing its truth due to biblical principles. I was expecting, "God would not work in that way" or some similar response. Instead it was embraced and encouraged that I continue. This taught me I should never be afraid to share my testimony with anyone, no matter what the outcome may be. A strong biblical message in Psalm 96:3 says, *"Declare his glory among the heathen, his wonders among all people."* I think that evening and its outcome helped to plant the seed you are reading now. A way to share my testimony that may lead even one person closer to knowing Jesus Christ. Do you have a testimony you should be sharing? We all do.

Thoughts of the cabin drifted into my head as spring approached; it was April 2017. Soon, the road to Winfield would be open, and I could take my bride to be there for the first time. It would be the first time ever that I had been to the cabin and had no alcohol in my system, stone-cold sober. I was excited about it. It was important to me and to her because where it all started is a large part of my testimony. I was anxious to show her the clues Charlie had left for me. Thoughts of the parables were in my head, and I needed to make sure the first visit showed no trace of the old life.

There was a problem, the cabin was for years Winfield Willy's Bar and Grill. It was now closed by order of Jesus Christ, but the liquor, beer, and wine were still there along with the tools to serve it up. I had to prepare before I could take her there for the first time. I needed to get rid of the booze. How to do this? My old way of thinking crept in, I could meet with one of my cabin drinking friends and simply give it all away. That would be easy. I would be done with it all in one big swoop.

"No way could I waste it all." Right? Sheila Joe encouraged me to pray about this. I know now she already knew what the right thing to do would be but wanted me to come to it using my newfound ways. This was one of the first decisions I made based on the Bible, Romans 14:13 says, *"Let us not therefore judge one another anymore: but judge this rather, that no man put a stumbling block or an occasion to fall in his brother's way."* I could plainly see what alcohol had done to my life; It was a clear blockade to any spiritual connection with God, it was poison to the body and soul, not only to me, but to all those around me. I had already decided it had to go from my life. Why would I give it to another person and perpetuate any desire they might have to consume it? I would be doing harm in a secondhand way but harm, nonetheless. I needed to *pour it out,* dispose of it totally. It was the right thing, and it was plain to see after prayer and reading God's Word.

One of the liquor supplies at Winfield Willy Bar and Grill about to go away.

Sheila Joe and I had a conversation and agreed, it would be best if I went at the first opportunity to get the job done, but Sheila Joe thought it best for me to not go it alone because my new sobriety and my new Christian beliefs had not had time to become my normal way. I needed strength; my plan was to go with God for spiritual strength and ask Pastor Bigler to help me physically. He loves the mountains as I do, and I knew a Baptist pastor would jump at the chance to deal a blow to Satan in such a way. He readily accepted my invitation, and the plan was set. It would be the first weekend in May 2017 when the bar in Winfield would permanently close and all traces would be disposed of. The big weekend came, and I was excited to get to Winfield but afraid of the unknown events and wondering how I would feel. Drinking had been the way I lived my entire adult life, so this was big change.

Traveling up with Pastor became a rolling Bible study for sure; he is a man of great wisdom, and he helped me know all would be well. All I needed to do was trust in Jesus and ask for strength. It would be given, I did, and it was. I had no trouble at all pouring out every drop into our fire pit, we figured about $4,000 worth. It felt great; this was booze that could harm no one now.

Pouring it out. Now it could harm no one.

A good decision had been made, and a huge victory had been claimed in the name of Jesus. We disposed of everything, glasses, towels, spoons, everything went in the trash. It is hard to describe how this felt after having been a hard-core alcoholic and watching addiction take Glenna's life and destroy my own. The power Jesus gave me over it is indescribable; it was given only by God's grace through faith in Jesus Christ. A true victory had been won.

The very next trip would be Sheila Joe's first. I asked Pastor if we could spend the night there, you know, adult Christians, able to abstain from any actions that could compromise our plan of abstinence. Being as wise as he is, he quoted scripture as an answer. Read 1 Thessalonians 5:22, it says, *"Abstain from all appearance of evil."* Wow, that spelled it out. Another truth is if it looks bad, it will be perceived as bad, no matter how pure it may be. Our first trip was an up and back day trip as it needed to be. As we planned our wedding and took part in the counseling with Pastor, I started to understand more about the Word of God and to understand Him.

People around me began to notice the difference in me, they would ask if I cared for a drink or suggested, "Let's go have a few" or put down their wife in conversation. Swearing began to leave me, and it irritated me when others would belt out expletives. I withdrew from any circumstance that involved these things. At first, I was reluctant to let people around me know *why* there had been a change in me. Not that I was ashamed, I just did not know how to do it, afraid I would be questioned and have no answers. Pastor and I had been praying during our studies, and I heard the other men in the church pray during services. Sheila Joe and I prayed about nearly everything; I was learning to talk to God.

Pastor is a great teacher; he knew just when and how I needed to move forward. He preached on the next parable found in Matthew 5:14-16, it says, *"Ye are the light of the world. A city that is set on a hill cannot be hid. Neither do men light a candle, and put it under a bushel, but on a candlestick; and it giveth light unto all that are in the house. Let your light so shine before men, that they may see your good works, and glorify your Father which is in heaven."* The next

Sunday, he asked me if I was ready to pray in church. I was, and I did. The parable tells me that now that I am saved, I should boldly tell people what had happened to me, spread the light, and share the Word at every opportunity and not hide it from all who ask but show it and tell it. Praying in church broke the ice for me. The lessons taught to me in these three simple parables are easy for me to remember. Pour out the old me, get rid of the sinful ways of acting and thinking. Pour in the new spirit, now that the old is gone there is plenty of room for the new. It is a gift from God, all I needed to do was let Him in. Finally, full of the new me, the new spirit. Let it overflow, pour it out to any who will listen and to those who will not listen right now. I always do this by letting the light in me shine in all directions. I do not need to be perfect at it, progression, not perfection, is the goal. Just keep on doing it. *Pour, pour, pour.*

Chapter 9
THE PINK CLOUD

WHY ARE YOU STILL READING THIS book? It may be that you are or were an addict like me, and you are able to relate your times of agony to mine. Perhaps life is hard for some other reason. Are you are looking for a way out and you are starting to see one on these pages? It may be that you are lost and are wondering about this God fellow like I was but are not sure how or where to find him. It may be that you are saved and just wanted to see another point of view. It may be that you are a biblical scholar and just want to scrutinize the way others think. It could be that you saw the snappy cover and had some free time in the airport.

I hope it is because without regard to why you picked up this book and started reading it, the words here have sparked something in you to make you realize that Father God, Jesus Christ, and the Holy Spirit are real, and you need them in your life and the way to find and understand how. It is simple. It does not matter if you are the worst of the worst or the best of the best, stoned or sober, *Paying Attention* is all you need to do. You may recall, at the beginning of this book, my goal was, and still is, to make a difference in someone's life, anyone's life. My desire is to bring one, even just one, person closer to knowing Jesus Christ as their Savior. Anything beyond one is a bonus in my eyes. This makes God happy according to Luke 15:10, it says,

"Likewise, I say unto you, there is joy in the presence of the angels of God over one sinner that repenteth." Because you are still reading, I pray you are that one or one of the ones. I do not know why you are still reading these pages, only you do. Are you *Paying Attention?*

All the hard work to get me sober has been done now, right? The shakes, mini strokes, heart palpitations, vomiting, diarrhea, hot and cold sweats, loss of appetite, dizziness, confusion, skin rashes, headaches, insomnia, medical screenings, counseling, embarrassment, and incarceration are in the past. Addiction was gone, just like that. After so many years of alcoholism, with all my hard work in the last few months, I was cured. I had found Jesus Christ as my Savior, the Holy Spirit had entered me, and I was saved. I had basic understanding of God, and I was certain I was safe at last, no more worry, no more sadness, and no more pain.

I had fallen in love with Sheila Joe, and we were to be married in the near future. After what I had been through and done to others, I was especially relieved to know I was loveable. I was completely certain at one point that I was not, but Sheila Joe believed in me and she helped me to do the same. God had brought us together through the oddest of circumstance, and we were blessed beyond belief. I had survived addiction surprisingly well. According to my doctor, I had some healing to do but was well underway to a normal checkup.

The good life was laid out in front of me like a red carpet. all I needed to do was move forward, the *pink cloud* had arrived. Sheila Joe and I both had high expectations for life and for each other, for our future together. I was about to learn that expectations are resentments in training. Right? Not sure this should be here, but our first year was hard for us both, and it needs to be in the book.

The term *"pink cloud"* is used in self-help addiction recovery meetings all over the world, and it was used in the ones I attended as well. It describes a false sense of security as to one's early addiction. If you have been there, you will know exactly what I am speaking of. I think mine was as a result of the relief that came with the little bits of victory I was beginning to achieve. The cloud of alcoholism was beginning to clear; I could eat, and I could sleep for more than an hour at a time. I could put more than two or three thoughts together at a time and felt like I had won. I could say, I got this, or I am cured with great confidence.

Looking back, I think mine was compounded three-fold. I was sober, I was saved, and I was in love. Wow, could things get any better? The powers to be in my self-help meetings warned of this; they said, "Concentrate on your recovery, or you will slip back into addiction." No major life changes were advised unless required to survive. If you had a job, keep it. If you had a roof over your head, do not move. If you were single, stay that way. I had the pink cloud to protect me, so I broke all these rules. When anyone would ask, "How are you?" my response would be, Invincible and I believed it. Right?

There is good news and bad news in sobriety. The good news is you begin to feel emotions again; the bad news is, you begin to feel emotions again. The double-edge sword comes out of its scabbard, sharp on both sides to be sure. For every action, there is a reaction. This was to be the next phase in early sobriety. My determination was to be tested. The pink cloud is a good thing, a great feeling, a natural high, if you will allow me. The pink cloud only lasted for a short while.

Then, PAWS snuck into my world: Post Alcohol Withdrawal Syndrome. PAWS is the other end of the pendulum swing. It happens to many around the one-year sober mark; it is an addict's brain not wanting to get rewired. My old friend alcohol, cunning, baffling, powerful, and patient, would put up one final fight to retain control of me. The syndrome has many physical symptoms, but for me most were in my mind. The biggest symptom is it dissipates the pink cloud immediately. *POOF*, things are hard again.

Doubt sets in, can I do this? Am I worthy of sobriety, let alone God's love? There is physical sobriety; this is simply not to drink. PAWS is the changing over of the wiring in the mind from intoxication to sobriety, emotional sobriety it is called. Learning how to react to situations that once baffled me, learning to react to any given situation as a normal, sober person would. It is the real hard mental part of learning to live day to day and to take life as it comes. I realized life was getting back to normal, the bills still had to be paid, clients were still aggravating, people still passed away, and life just keep coming, sober or not.

I had to deal with life on life's terms, all of it for the first time in my life with any degree of sobriety. I began to rely my sobriety and the love I had for my wife rather than on Jesus Christ, which was a mistake. Sheila Joe and Pastor reminded me these things were not what I should look to for guidance as a Christian. I realized I needed to go to the Bible for guidance. My new bride and I went through this together, and it was a huge challenge early in our marriage. I admire her more than I can say here and now. We had started to go to a Friday night Bible study at this point. At one of the very first studies, we were reading Luke 6:46-49, it says,

> *"And why call ye me, Lord, Lord, and do not the things which I say? Whosoever cometh to me, and heareth my sayings , and doeth them, I will shew you to whom he is like: He is like a man which built an house, and digged*

deep, and laid the foundation on a rock: and when the flood arose, the stream beat vehemently upon that house, and could not shake it: it was founded upon a rock. But he that heareth, and doeth not, is like a man that without a foundation built an house upon the earth; against which the stream did beat vehemently, and immediately it fell; and the ruin of that house was great."

This was the fourth parable that hit me, what was being taught is that Jesus is not asking us to listen to what He says or admire Him or be impressed. He is saying "Do what I say, or all professions of repentance mean nothing." I knew what I needed to do. My base of belief needed to be built on the solid rock, the Word of God, not things of this earth. Reading and understanding were a great start, but we also need to be doers of His Word. I picked out two verses to start with; mastering just these two simple principles could and would make a huge difference in my world and in every relationship I was involved in, especially my marriage. James 1:22 says, *"But be ye doers of the word, and not hearers only, deceiving your own selves,"* and James 1:19, *"Wherefore, my beloved brethren, let every man be swift to hear, slow to speak, slow to wrath."*

I prayed for the ability to apply this verse to myself, to be a doer of the Word and to control my emotions. It seemed to me that the entire world is set up to make it harder to follow God's Word than our own feelings. A man who has his foundation firmly on the rock, Jesus Christ, will have a much easier time getting to the right thing.

Like I said in the beginning of this chapter, there is a reason you are still reading. Only you know what that reason is, but one thing I am positive about is your reason has something to do with the Bible, right? Do you own a Bible? If you do, find it and make sure it is in your hand. If you don't, go buy one or borrow one; no matter how you do it, get a Bible in your hand. You will be amazed how far down the road toward a true spiritual connection with Jesus Christ simply holding God's Word in your hand will take you. This is a call to action, if you have even the smallest inkling that you need Jesus Christ in your life, and you do, by the way.

The tiniest urge to move toward God, did you just blink? Did you just take a deep breath? Did you just shudder or get a chill up your spine? Even if you just thought for one split second you may want and need forgiveness of all your sins and eternal life, if you want to be able to let it all go, be full of forgiveness and love and truly know that God loves you, is that a tear? *Pay attention.* Stop reading this right now and get a Bible into your hand, literally, in your hand, *now*! Do it!

It feels amazing, doesn't it?

Now, I know you are in possession of a Bible because you just did what I asked you to do. Right? I can only offer my advice and share my experience, strength, and hope with you. I can tell you what it was like, how my life changed, what I personally did to change it, and what it is like now. We have all used the saying "You can lead a horse to water, but you cannot make him drink•" This applies here as well. I cannot force anyone to want to know Jesus Christ, and I certainly can't make anyone seek salvation. Open your Bible and turn to Ephesians 2:8-9, it says, *"For by grace are ye saved through faith; and that not of your own selves: it is the gift of God. Not of works, lest any man should boast."*

Grace is the unmerited favor of God; it cannot be bought or traded for, and it can't be worked for and earned; it is simply given by God. It is given through faith in God's son, Jesus Christ. That is it, the only way. Now read John 3:16, it says, *"For God so loved the world, that he gave his only begotten Son that whosoever believeth in Him should not perish, but have everlasting life."* Do you believe it? Do you have faith? Do you want to believe? Hebrews 11:1 says, *"Now faith is the substance of things hoped for, the evidence of things not seen."* Faith comes in different levels as I see it. Each breath we take is faith based; without a thought, we have faith the air will not poison us. The same applies to a drink of water or a bite of food. Do you believe the sun will come up tomorrow? This is faith in God's creation for sure, unless you still have absolutely nothing on your evidence list. Is it not faith each and every time we drive our car through a green light, that the other drivers will stop on their red?

Faith gets bigger in certain circumstances doesn't it? How about when we go in for an operation? Fear is there, but we know the outcome will make better or perhaps even save our life, or we could just not make it. Faith tells us we will survive. This is faith in small terms. The Bible tells us faith the size of a mustard seed, properly applied, will have the power to move mountains. How do we learn to have this kind of faith? Romans 10:17 gives us the answer, it says, *"So the faith cometh by hearing, and hearing by the Word of God."*

I ask you to be a doer and read Hebrews 11, start to finish, and consider how much faith the people described must have had. How can a person eat an elephant? One bite at a time. I am learning faith in the same way. After reading *Hebrews 11*, start tomorrow and read your Bible every day. Any little bit is a start. I use the time to read, I once used to think about, find, consume, and recover from alcohol. I have plenty of time; how about you? Second Corinthians 5:7 says, *"For we walk by faith, and not by sight."*

Chapter 10
SIN IS SIN

O KAY, SO LET ME GET STARTED ON this next chapter. This is the first chapter I am really struggling with as far as how to say what I want to say. So, I guess I will just say it in whatever way comes flowing out of my brain and hope it makes sense in the end. Keep in mind, I am not a biblical scholar; I am just a regular guy with regular problems wanting to live a better life through Jesus Christ. Progression not perfection. This one is hard.

The Bible tells me the reason I feel the way I feel is because of my sin and guilt from sin. Sin started way back when, by Adam and Eve in the Garden of Eden. By eating the forbidden fruit, they broke God's rules, right? How did I get mixed up in this sin business then? It is because man has had a broken relationship with God from that moment on. God has rules and we all break them just like Adam and Eve did. Because by nature, I am a sinner; we all are. Sin comes from within me because I was born this way. Humans can be brutal; in order to get what we want; some will do anything. We will steal, cheat, even kill to get what we want. All of these are sins.

Am I big sinner or a little sinner, I had to know? Is there a difference? I always thought there were different levels of sin, like traffic tickets, rolling through a stop sign was bad, and a ticket could be issued if I were caught. On the flip side, when

I was caught driving under the influence, even though it was a prescription drug taken as directed, I was put in handcuffs and taken to jail. Multiple offenses could have gotten me a long prison sentence. If I caused an accident and someone was killed, I would have been convicted of murder and locked up for life. There is a big difference in the crimes and the severity of punishment for the crimes.

Using this train of thought, stealing a candy bar or telling a white lie was a small sin and would mostly be overlooked by God. Killing another man would be a huge sin and dealt with severely. Not so. The Bible tells me in James 2:10-11, it says, *"For whosoever shall keep the whole law, and yet offend in one, he is guilty of all. Sin is sin, it is all equal in God's eyes."* Romans 6:23 says, *"For the wages of sin is death, but the gift of God is eternal life in Jesus Christ our lord."* The things it does not say make it clear to me that the wages of sin *is* death, cut and dried; it does not say some sin or maybe or sometimes. The wages of sin *is* death.

Let us go back to the getting caught part of the traffic ticket scenario. There is a big "if" involved, isn't there? If there is a policeman there and happens to see me and decides to enforce the law, I could get a ticket. The reality is that the chance of getting caught is ridiculously small and the chance of getting a ticket even smaller. There are drivers, like my wife Sheila Joe, who roll through dozens of *stop signs* every year and never get a ticket. She simply relies on the low probability of getting caught. Now let us apply more scripture. First John 3:20 says, *"For if our heart condemns us, God is greater than our heart, and knoweth all things."* I understand this to mean when I commit a sin, I know I did, and because God is omnipresent, He knows I did and was sitting next to me in the front seat while I did. There are no secret cameras to hide from, no chance God is not looking. I did it and I am caught.

Now I know sin is sin and when I sin God knows, and the wage of sin is death. So why do I still sin? Why do any of us still sin? I can only speak for me when I say some sin is easy to avoid, willful sin, so to speak. I would never kill anyone or commit adultery or rob a bank; I just would not. It is the heart and mind that must be mastered to be as close as possible to sin free, to live God's way.

I must learn exactly what sin is if I am to avoid it, this comes through reading and the study of the Word of God. There is no complete list of sins in the Bible. They are there, just not all in one place in alphabetical order. We must search them out to learn. It would be nice to have a checklist in my cell phone Bible app. I could hold the phone up to my forehead, think the thought, and it could tell me a yes or a no. Nice, but it does not work that way.

There are lots of sins mentioned, described, and discussed in the Bible, but no "complete list of sins." I must know what sin is in my heart. We are all taught the difference between right and wrong throughout our lives; most of these lessons are plain to see. Matthew 7:12 says, *"Therefore all things whatsoever ye would so that men should do to you, do ye even so to them: for this is the law and the prophets."* Do unto others as you would have them do unto you, in other words—a common one we all know. If it feels like it is wrong, it is, and I know it. A better description may be to ask myself if I can and will ask God to bless my thought or action. If not, it is probably a sin; the key is to ask in advance. The reason behind the thought or action will cause it to be a sin as well, whether pride, greed, lust, spite, envy, selfishness, manipulation, or any other thoughts of ill will toward another.

Remember, God knows all our thoughts as well. I believe sin is anything that troubles me in my conscience. When this happens, I need to *Pay Attention* because it is Jesus Christ wanting to work in my life. Have you chosen the wrong path in life and wish you could have what you did or said removed from your burden? Are you an addict like me? Do you have a sin eating at you?

What is "it? Ask yourself; Jesus already knows and is ready to remove your sin. All these things can and will be removed from you when you ask Jesus Christ to be your Savior. They were from me. There is no right or wrong set of words that will do this; it is not the words that matter here but the belief in your heart. Pray to God as your Creator, admit you are a sinner, believe that Jesus Christ died on the cross for your sins and was buried and rose again from death on the third day. Tell Him you believe in His Word and ask Jesus to come into your heart and accept Him as your Lord and Savior. You will feel it when the Holy Spirit enters you, and it will happen right then and there. Just like that you are forgiven.

You are a child of God now. Jesus told many as in John 8-1 saying to "Go *and sin no more.*" I try hard every day to live in a way that will please God, but, like me, you will sin every day; we all do. The beautiful thing about it is we truly are forgiven by God the moment we get saved; the past, present, and future sin is all forgiven now. This does not give us a license to go out and commit sins at will; we must be humble and have Jesus in our heart. God wants us to live by His Word now, and you have the power in you provided by the Holy Spirt through prayer to do this.

Learn to pray; you now have the attention of the most powerful force ever. Really you do, and He loves you and has forgiven all your sins. Hebrews 4:16 says, *"Let us therefor come boldly unto the throne of grace, that we may obtain mercy, and find grace to help in time of need."* Pray for guidance and the wisdom to see His will for your life and the power to carry out His will. Jesus wants you to follow His teaching now. Hebrews 10:26 says, *"For if we sin willfully after we have received the knowledge of the truth, there remains no more sacrifice for sins."* It is explained in Galatians 5:16 it says, *"This I say then, walk in the spirit, and ye shall not fulfil the lust of the flesh."* Sin is defined in many places many ways. This is why it is so hard to figure out for a regular guy like me. It is simple, but it is not. When I *Pay Attention* in my heart to the Holy Spirit within me, choices become obvious as to God's will for me. I simply need to follow.

God's Word says our forgiveness needs to pass on to others; it is one of His requirements for receiving His forgiveness. Matthew 6:14-15 says, *"For if ye forgive men their trespasses, your heavenly father will also forgive you. But if ye forgive not their trespasses, neither will your father forgive your trespasses."* Again, God wants his children to follow His Word. The message is clear, God forgave me; therefore, I am to forgive others.

The truths about forgiveness are spelled out plainly in these few verses. It had to be done this way so it would be easy for me to understand and apply:

Romans 3:23 says, *"For all have sinned, and come short of the glory of God."* We all need His forgiveness, all of us. Just consider the forgiveness you have been shown by grace.

Acts 7:59-60 says, *"And they stoned Stephen, calling upon God, and saying, Lord Jesus, receive my spirit. And he kneeled down, and cried with a loud voice, Lord lay not this sin to their charge, and when he had said this, he fell asleep."* We are to forgive those who do not deserve it; can you forgive someone in your life, who does not deserve your forgiveness? Luke 23:34 says, *"Forgive them Father for they know not what they do."* Spoken by Jesus as he is crucified. God has forgiven us by His grace.

Matthew 18:22 says, "Jesus saith unto him, I say not unto thee, Until seven times: but Until seventy times seven." I am to forgive with no limit, over and over. God has no final straw, no limit, no that is it, and I shouldn't either. This may seem impossible, but if I am *"Paying Attention"* to the Holy Spirit and believe all things are possible with God, then I can do this. We sometimes need to forgive, then love from a distance. Resentments only spoil the joy God gives us. Will I let it go?

Psalm 139:23 says, *"Search me, my God, and know my heart: try me, and know my thoughts:"* We can't fool God; He knows if we have forgiven others truly in our hearts. Take it seriously, pray for the strength to forgive. The Holy Spirit is already inside you and will give you the power to forgive. Really forgive, we must.

Ephesians 4:32 exhorts us to, *"And be ye kind to one another, tenderhearted, forgiving one another, even as God for Christs sake hath forgiven you."* Forgiveness can be and is one of the most difficult thigs God asks us to do. But He also sets the example and sent His only son to die for all our sins so that we may be forgiven. Our debt is paid in full by Jesus Christ; therefore, God forgives us by His grace. Follow this example and forgive.

Another aspect of forgiveness in my heart is to seek the forgiveness of those I have wronged. If I am asking God to forgive me for things I have done to others, then I must also reconcile with the people themselves if I am to receive God's full blessings. Matthew 5:23-24 says, *"Therefore if you bring thy gift to the altar, and there rememberest that thy brother hath ought against you; Leave there thy gift before the altar, and go thy way; first be reconciled to thy brother, and then come and offer thy gift."* Yes, this means saying, "I was wrong, and I am sorry for what I did to you." It is hard to do, mainly because in my case, they may not accept my apology or my efforts to make amends. The offended could get mad and retaliate because an old wound could be reopened. I believe it is especially hard for an addict because we are so self-centered and for such a long time, we were certain we were right and everyone else was wrong.

It takes two to tango, so to speak, and if there is anger between two, then the Bible tells me to reach out and ask forgiveness and forgive as well. Should I not receive their forgiveness after letting them know I regret it and apologize, then the burden is theirs; it is no longer mine. I have asked for and received forgiveness from many I harmed along the way, and I make a daily examination of anyone I may have offended or harmed that day and make an amends promptly. This way I avoid creating any new hurt in the ones I know and love. The hardest amends I needed to make by far was to Glenna, but how? She was gone from this earth. I decided to writer her a letter.

The letter was handwritten in the early springtime of 2018 on the table at the cabin. The letter told her I was sorry for all the things I had done to contribute to her alcoholism, the wrongs I had done to her, and all the unchristian things I had said over the years. I asked her for her forgiveness. I had kept back some ashes from being spread at her service for some reason. Now I knew why. They were in the beautiful alabaster box decorated with ivory trout and bears. I placed the letter in the box along with the wilted rose from that day, the sermon written by Uncle Roger, and a note I put there.

I do not remember writing the note and was surprised when I found it there. I took the box to a spot where a faint trail leads to a waterfall she liked to go to. I placed the box on a rock so the morning sun would warm it and when the spring runoff started, it would be taken away. I said a prayer for her and my goodbyes, and walked away, feeling I had done my part according to God's Word. My burden was lifted.

Someone told me, "You need to forgive yourself." Wow, I began to think about it, and I sure had a lot to forgive myself for. Glenna's death was my fault according to the doctor because of my addiction. The damage I caused others because of it was most certainly my fault. I cannot remember all the evil things I did in the past. Was this a new issue on top of getting sober and cleaning up my life?

I began to look where I knew the answer would be: God's Word. I looked intently for any scripture to help me know what God wanted me to know about self-forgiveness, and I could not find it. Why? It is not there. How silly it would be if we had to forgive ourselves? Why not go out and sin all we wanted, then forgive ourselves, start over, and go sin some more, nope.

God had already given me His forgiveness. How could I possibly be so self-centered to think my forgiveness on top of His was even necessary. In fact, the thought of self-forgiveness is not for the children of God but really would boil down to heresy. God's forgiveness cannot be added to, improved on, or enhanced in any way. It is divine, perfect, and absolute forgiveness. Now that I have been forgiven by God, there is nothing left to forgive. Ephesians 2:8-9 says, *"For by grace ye are saved through faith; and that not of yourselves: it is the gift of God. Not of works, lest any man should boast."*

Accepting God's forgiveness is hard. I think it is because I am so self-centered and prideful. I have this vision of myself as a kind, loving, caring person. A bad case of terminal uniqueness lived in me before I asked Jesus into my heart. I could never do something like that and freely admit it, so I could not truly admit I did it in the first place. Whatever my deed was, it just would not leave me alone; it kept reappearing in my heart and in my conscience. Being a new Christian, this is something I struggle with. What it does say in the Bible over and over is I am forgiven by grace, 1 John 1:9 tells me, *"If we confess our sins, He is faithful and just to forgive us our sins, and cleanse us from all uprightness."*

This is the same kind of love an earthly father has for his children. He knows his children will make mistakes along the way, some by accident and some on purpose. It does not matter; our fathers still love us if they know Christ. The reason I still need to ask for forgiveness every day through prayer is to show God I trust Him fully with my heart, to obtain an intimate relationship with Him, to gain His blessings, and to be present with God and reaffirm I need Him. In my simple way of thinking, it's like showing up for work every day; it proves you want and need your job. I believe by reading God's Word every day and showing up in God's presence every day in prayer, I can live a life of peace within. It takes practice for me, but I know all things are possible with God. Matthew 19:26 says, *"But Jesus beheld them, and said unto them, with men this is impossible; but with God all things are possible."* Progression, not perfection.

Chapter 11
FRIEND OR FOE

FRIENDS HAVE ALWAYS BEEN A HUGE source of satisfaction and at the same time a huge source of frustration in my world. We have all had those friends that would be our best friend until the end. There is one who fills that need for sure; that one is Christ. John 15:13 says, *"Greater love hath no man than this, that a man lay down his life for his friends"*. Jesus did just that on the cross for us all. As far back as I can remember, I had earthly friends. I even had blood brothers, just like in an old movie.

Then because of one reason or another, we seemed to lose track of one another. When we were kids, our moms and dads moved away; we went to different schools, got married, went to work, and made new friends. Perhaps our best friend stole a friend or worse yet, a boyfriend or girlfriend, bad news for friendship. Then as we get older, life happens, and things simply change. I have been blessed with many true friends over the years, some I thought would be for life, but few were. The best friend I ever had and still have is Terrye Clear. Our friendship started way back in the early eighties. We both worked at the same place, and being ten years older than I was, he held a much better position. I was a wash rack man in the back, a laborer sort of job. I got dirty, wet, and cold. Terrye sat up front in a warm office and had a company truck to drive, more pay, and better benefits. Personally, he had a beautiful wife and great, athletic, smart daughters and a nice home. Truly, I was jealous of him and what he had. We both loved to hunt, but he had stopped because of a hunting accident that took the life of a close friend of his, crushing him emotionally and he just stopped.

One day, I asked T.C. as I called him, why he had all the good stuff and I seemed to just be floundering in life. He said, "Close the door, sit down, shut up, and listen." He told me exactly what I needed to do, and I listened. He told me I needed to stop with "F" bombs every time I opened my mouth, learn to read and write, and clean up my person for starters. I did, and he became a friend, a brother, and a father figure all in one. I looked up to him then, and I do to this day. I have been listening to and taking heed of his advice for decades now.

We became friends, and I convinced him to give hunting another try. He did, and in no time at all, we were the best of friends. Terrye has always been honest with me, supported me when he could, and told me when he could not. We started and ran a business for over a decade, and even though we did not always agree, we always had respect for one another and had each other's backs. We worked and played, mixed in with hard and good times of life. The best times were centered around activities, of course, hunting, fishing, golf, cabin time, boating, and whatever was on stage at the time.

But the hard things grew us as well. T.C. knew I drank too much even back then, and I know he could see the trouble on the horizon, but he has always been there for me. Along the way, I misplaced him somehow; he does not drink, so our agendas were much different. We stayed in touch and had lunch every now and then. I never realized he was leading me and loving me until after I was saved. I think he knows God is always on time and was waiting for me to be ready and receptive for a Christian friendship.

Psalm 27:14 says, *"Wait for the Lord; be strong, and let your heart take courage; wait for the Lord."* He told me at one of our last lunch meetings toward the end of my addiction he had accepted Jesus Christ as his Savior six or seven years before. I did not know what that meant at the time, I could tell something was different within him, but exactly what it was, I could not see through the fog. As my addiction became worse, the less I wanted or needed company. I still did many of the same activities but alone—no wife, no friend, nobody. The last decade or so centered around my drinking habit and my drinking habit alone.

The enjoyment began to fade from the things I once loved to do: hunting, fishing, boating, golf you name it, anything outside, warm or cold, wet or dry, go, go, go. I drank no matter what I was doing, of course. Then, slowly, everything became less about the activity and more about the drink. Then, finally it became all about the drinking and not at all about the activity. During this decade of decline, the bar was always open, and the drinks were on the house. I was the house.

Drinking was my main thing all day, every day, at this point. This was true both at The Dusty Buffalo Saloon in my home in Pueblo West and at Winfield Willy's Bar and Grill. Many of my friends and family looked at my home as a free bar all the time. Birds of a feather flock together. When work was over and home seemed to hard a place to go, The Dusty Buffalo was a handy pit stop and the price was low, no free. Most evenings we had company of some kind, friend or family. Glenna and I were all in, we were also guilty. We loved to pour the drinks and be the center of attention.

Most nights, the appetizers were prepared, and the party usually went until someone's wife called and was agitated because dinner was cold at home and the kids were in bed. Then, when the party was over, we made sure, and so did they, a road drink was in their hand to hold them over on the drive home. The bar was well stocked with all the high-end liquors, wines, beers, and mixers. I am certain the drinks were better and stronger than any bar or at their own homes. Many wives scolded me more than once, and I know several frequent visitors were banned from my house. It was worse at the cabin; I am sure it is because no one had to get up and go to work the next day. It was play time, party time, all the time. The last couple of summers it was bad, neighbors would appear at the breakfast table, in heat of the day and at the evening campfire and they were thirsty. I remember walking into my cabin seeing people I didn't even know drinking in my kitchen; we made friends very quickly, right?

The Dusty Buffalo Saloon closed when we lost that home in 2010, but it was moved to the next place where we lived on Coral Drive. We lost much, but not the booze. The sign and the inventory were moved, and the party raged on. Winfield Willy's Bar at the cabin remained open until the end. Don't get me wrong, I was all in and loved every minute of it. I liked being the *man of the hour*. I loved it when neighbors would say what an awesome party we put on. I was a legend in my own mind.

Eventually the drink took over completely, and I became a solitary drinker, even preferring to be away from the closest friends; even Glenna became a hindrance to my addiction, and mine became a hindrance to her. I think this was part of the reason we separated. If we drank together, it resulted in a fight. At least drinking alone was quiet. I drank alone and occasionally with one of the few real hard-core alcoholics I called friends, not for conversation or enjoyment, just to get drunk. Looking back, I regret this with all my heart. I need to accept the forgiveness of

Jesus on this, and I accept fully the responsibility for the harm I caused to my family and friends, including countless hangovers, marital fights, family feuds, sleepless nights, emergency room visits, and the contribution to long-term health issues and even death to some. Death to some still to come that are stuck in their own addiction that I contributed to. I know what I am looking at now, and it is plain to see in several friends of my time before sobriety.

I never felt so alone after I sobered up. The few true friends were still there and were very sympathetic and helpful. I wasn't there for them like I should have been. They saved me from myself. I was invited to many functions but soon became aware of how different life would be now—in a good but hard way. No longer drinking left me with no sober social skills. I had no desire to drink and did not care to be around people who were, probably because I could see my old self reflected in them. I tried a few gatherings and was just really the odd man out. My party mode was, in the corner away from the crowd and quiet. I was hiding more than anything.

For what seemed like a lifetime, I went to work, went to my rehab meetings and classes, and went home. I was very lonesome. I knew solitude was a huge enemy of my sobriety but was unsure what to do. I know I did some foxhole praying at that time, asking God to fix this and get me where I wanted to go. I was now ready to cut my own deal with Him. I knew He was there, but I did not yet know Him or how to communicate with Him. This went on through the holidays that year. Christmas was my first sober Christmas ever as an adult, alone and hard, and the New Year celebrations were much the same. I went on into the new year, just being alone most of the time. This was all part of God's plan for me as I see it now. The experience at the cabin still had me searching for God with no clue how or where to find him.

Had there been a lot of friends around at the time, especially old friends doing the old things, it would have had a terribly negative impact on my new sobriety and my search for God. There was a definite void in the friend department of my life when sister Cheryl first gave me Sheila Joe's phone number. This in turn, would lead me to make the call to her, and that is what took me one step closer to Jesus Christ. I believe this was all by God's design. Then because of the grace of God, I was saved. My remaining friends became scarce, not because we were no longer friends, they had saved me once and would do anything for me, and I would do the same for them.

The deep bond was still there and is to this day. It is just way different now. I see the difficulty in them, when a swear word slips out and the attached head snaps in my direction, looking to gage my reaction, kind of an whoops face looking at me. Not that there is a reaction, but the perception is that there would be. I have had friends offer me a cocktail, then give the same look, like, "Oh man, have I offended Bill?" I cannot think of one single friend that has made any attempt to avoid contact at Walmart or anything. It is just a more distant friendship, from a distance, An I don't understand you any more kind of friendship.

There is no blame on my part either. I am the one who changed, and as my beliefs became stronger and I sought spiritual guidance, it became clearer as to how I needed to act to fall in line with God's wishes, not in a judgmental way toward friends and acquaintances, just in a way that pleased God according to His Word. 1 Corinthians 5:9-13 says,

*"I wrote unto you in an epistle not to company with forni-
cators: yet not altogether with the fornicators of this world,
or with the covetous, or extortioners, or with idolaters; for
then must ye needs go out of the world. But now I have
written unto you not to keep company, if any man that is
called a brother be a fornicator, or covetous, or an idolater,
or a railer, or a drunkard, or an extortioner; with such an
one no not to eat. For what have I to do to judge also them
that are without? do not ye judge them that are within?
But them that are without God judgeth. Therefore, put
away from among yourselves that wicked person."*

This tells me I am to separate myself from these people and
leave the judging to God. The more I learned the less I missed
the sin that I now recognize as sin. Ephesians 5:11 says, *"Take
no part in unfruitful works of darkness, but instead expose them"*. This
tells me I need not be present where these things take place; I
pray by my not being there, it may be exposed in conversation
as to why I am absent.

Now, I don't know if he had heard some rumors that I had
survived or if this was just a God thing, But the phone rang,
and it was my old faithful friend Terrye Clear. It was great to
hear from him, and now I knew what was different. We were
brothers in Christ, amazing! We had come full circle. I was
really excited to introduce Sheila Joe to Terrye and his wife,
Nancy, so a lunch was planned. We had a long history and had
been through much together, so I wanted them to be part of
this new life, and I could see that as Christians it would be a
much different path.

The lunch went well, and Nancy and Sheila Joe seemed
especially pleased with each other. Terrye and Nancy were both
as excited about my salvation as I am. They wanted to hear this

testimony, and I wanted to share it, so we planned a time down the road to get back together. What a time it would turn out to be. They became a part of the testimony. The day came, and we went to the Clear's home early so I could share this testimony with them; then we planned to go out to eat.

We gathered in the living room, and the testimony began. I told it as it is in this book, and all listened intently and had much the same reactions other Christians had had as key points came to the surface. Some questions and comments were made as we moved through it. As the end neared and the date of my salvation came to the surface, Terrye became very intense, He said "What day was that?" I said it was a Thursday. He almost interrupted me and said, "No, what date?" What date did you get saved? He was insistent, "what day?" He wanted to know right then. So, I repeated the date: February 23, 2017. He became very emotional and with a tear in his eyes, he spoke. "You are not going to believe this," He told his own story about that same day.

He began by letting us know February 23, 2017, was a big day in his life as well. Seems he had been to see his doctor that day, and the news was not good. He was told he has a life-taking disease. Needless to say, that night was restless for him. He finally went to sleep but sometime in the night, a dream came to him. In the dream, I was locked in a room with two people from our past, very evil people, no names, just Satan in the flesh. Both men had done unspeakable things, and Terrye and I were heavily involved in bringing what they had done to the light of day. It had caused a huge mess in many lives long ago.

Terrye said in the dream, he could see in a small window into the room, and all he could see was turmoil and chaos, wind, lights flashing, fire, my screams of pain, spinning and shaking inside. There was a door, and he wanted desperately to open it and help me, but it was locked and no matter how hard he tried, it would not budge, though he was yanking and pulling.

Terrye, begged God to let him in so he could help me, and at that moment, an empty wooden chair sitting by the door slid back against the wall as though someone had stood up abruptly and hit the chair with their knees. He heard a voice say, *"Fear not, I have him now; he is with me."* Terrye believes the Holy Spirit was sitting in the chair the whole time, and his prayer had been answered. Terrye felt calm and slept, not knowing I had accepted Jesus Christ as my Savior that very day. I do not profess to know how these things happen but by the grace of God, they do. God performs miracles every day, and I believe the connection Terrye and I have in Christ is another miracle, part of the mystery and huge on my evidence list. We are friends for life and beyond.

Work in the friend department is needed on my part, as Proverbs 18:24 says, *"A man that hath friends must shew himself friendly: and there is a friend that sticketh closer than a brother."* I am working on accepting God's calling to show myself more friendly, but progress is needed.

Chapter 12
THE MYSTERY

ONE OF THE REMAINING MYSTERIES IN this testimony is my lucky number; we all have one. Mine came from a date back when Terrye Clear and I sold our equipment rental company; it was the first time I remember needing to input my security code in a computer to gain access. It was about the time the data world changed, and everything required some level of security. It happened to be on the very day we closed the sale of the company: March 16, 1998. "Put in your code," they said. I didn't have one; it had to be four digits, so the date, *0316*, was the number I used. I have used it ever since then in one form or another, adding letters or characters as required for whatever any program required. I never thought this number would have anything to do with anything except being the closing date of this transaction way back when.

The mystery of the mountains.

As you may know, the best-known verse in the Bible world-wide and one of the most important ones is John 3:16, it says, *"For God so loved the world, he gave his only begotten Son, that whosoever believeth in Him should not perish, but have everlasting life."* This verse really sums up the message of salvation. It tells us how deep God's love is for us and the sacrifice He made so that our sins can be forgiven. The Bible tells us we are all separated from God because of sin. Romans 3:23-24 says, *"For all have sinned, and come short of the glory of God; Being justified freely by His grace through the redemption that is in Jesus Christ."* Can you imagine giving up any of your sons or any other person you love for others' sake, especially others who had repeatedly and consistently broken your own rules? But God loves us so much He made a way for us to have a way to redeem the relationship He wanted with us from the beginning of time. He also made it simple to find and follow this way. His own Son died on the cross to pay the cost of sin for us all with his own life, which is huge. Romans 6:23 says, *"For the wages of sin is death; but the gift of God is eternal life through Jesus Christ our Lord."* As in John 3:16 above, our sin debt was paid in full the very moment Jesus Christ died on the cross.

Of course, as I began to learn and study God's Word, this became one of my favorites as well. As this testimony unfolded, I began to see other New Testament 3:16 verses with significance; was this a clue to the mystery of Charlie Jones? First Timothy 3:16 says, *"And without controversy great is the mystery of godliness: God was manifest in the flesh, justified in the spirit, seen of angel, preached unto the gentiles, believed on in the world, received up into glory."* Fully God, fully human, born of a virgin, willing and able to face and overcome all the same temptations we face, Jesus felt all the pain we feel yet lived a perfect life free of sin.

Another is found in 2 Timothy 3:16, it says, *"All scripture is given by inspiration of God, and is profitable for doctrine, for reproof, for correction, for instruction in righteousness."* This verse reinforced my belief that the Bible is in fact the Word of God, written by men but authored by God. It is the ultimate direction for how we should aspire to live our lives. Biblical doctrine for me is like a vitamin I must take each day to set the stage for the day. Like a vitamin, it builds up in me over time, and I feel better when I take it and feel off if I don't. This is my morning meditations and readings; the more I read, the more I soak in and the quicker I can call on the energy it provides as needed throughout the day. I know if I don't take my Bible vitamin, I am off the entire day. It also helps me to identify my thoughts and actions that are not following God's Word and how to correct myself and know how to get back in line with God. It truly is the instruction manual of life, and if followed as close as possible, it will guide me to this better life I seek.

I must follow that up with verse 17, *"That the man of God may be perfect, thoroughly furnished unto all good works."* This tells me it is all I need; it is the complete guide to life. Imagine having the "how to" book of marriage, parenthood, finance, friendship, love, truth, health, frustration, anger, sex, honesty, addiction, and any other of life's challenges you may be facing. You do have it, it is all in your Bible.

As I read on, another one seemed to jump out at me. The story is told of Peter and John who went to the temple to worship. Acts 3:16 is what Peter said to the crowd after he healed a man who had been lame from birth and begged outside the temple each day. I think this one would have made a perfect answer for when people I knew back before I was saved by Jesus asked me "What happened to the old Bill"? It is a great description of what happened to me personally. I had been healed by Jesus and it was easy to see by any onlookers. Acts 3:16 says, *"By faith in the name of Jesus, this man who you see and know was made strong. It is Jesus' name and the faith that comes through him that has given this complete healing to him, as you can all see."* (From NIV Bible). Jesus can and does heal each day, and there are millions of people who have received the gift through faith. I also noticed the people who were healed by Jesus were healed to the degree they believed they would be.

So, what if they believed more; would they gave gotten more? I also see that Jesus never failed because He misjudged the faith of the person in need. He never did a halfway healing. All the people healed were healed to the full extent of the belief they had, so why not believe? Your healing may or may not be a physical healing but a head and heart healing. I know if the pain I felt inside from all I had been through can be healed by Him, yours can too. Simply believe it can, and it will, all the way. Because I do not believe in coincidence, 0316 had to be put into my life long ago for a specific reason. I now believe that like Charlie Jones, God, put it there knowing someday when my heart was open and ready to accept, Jesus, the 0316 in my life, would fall right into place and help me to become even more faithful throughout the rest of my life.

The final 0316 in the Bible, Revelation 3:16 says, *"So then because thou art lukewarm, and neither cold nor hot, I will spue thee out of my mouth."* This one tells me God wants us to be all in concerning our belief and faith in Jesus Christ, and the those who choose to set on the fence will not receive His blessings. I intend to be very warm in my spiritual life; I want to be near God, as near as possible. James 4:8 says, *"Draw nigh to God, and he will draw nigh to you. Cleanse your hands, ye sinners; and purify your hearts, ye double minded."* What is your lucky number?

There is the mention throughout the Bible of three and a half days, months, or years as a time frame, expressed as a time, times and a half as in Daniel 12:7, it says,

> *"And I heard the man clothed in linen, which was on the water of the river, when he held up his right hand and his left hand unto Heaven and swear by him that liveth forever that it shall be for a time, times and a half; and when he shall have accomplished to scatter the power of the holy people, all these things shall be finished."*

In some cases, forty-two months is the number, as in Revelation 13:5, it says, *"And he was given a mouth speaking great things and blasphemies, and he was given authority to continue for 42 months. "* In biblical times the calendar used was a lunar calendar, and it was based on twelve 30-day months each year or 360 days in a year, so three and one-half years would be 1,260 days, also mentioned in some verses. Hallie Dannenhauer lived here on earth for 1,284 days, or on our modern solar calendar, 3.51years. I will rely on a calendar expert to analyze this information and share their thoughts.

The reading I have done tells me biblical time has more of a symbolic meaning than an exact calculated meaning as in 2 Peter 3:8, it says, *"But, beloved, be not ignorant of this one thing, that one day is with the Lord as a thousand years, and a thousand years as one day."* So, it is close enough to cause me to think about it anyway? Now I don't know enough about how the calendar works now or in biblical times to debate the right or wrong of this calculation, but I do know in my heart it is part of the mystery held in my testimony. Why did this little girl live this length of time? What does it mean pertaining to my salvation, or perhaps yours? It took me about three and a half years from the time I first saw Charlie Jones on the mountain to the day I accepted Jesus Christ as my Savior; are you curious again? I know it is significant, and by faith it will be revealed to me when I need to know the how and why of this.

The Bible tells us about lots of miracles that God performed in biblical times, both large and small: parting the Red Sea, healing the lame, causing the blind to see, and many others. Then there are the small miracles that happen every day, even in today's world. We see them and hear about them from time to time. People who the doctors say have no chance at survival live. Terminal cancer is cured simply by faith and prayer, even smaller things like the homeless mother who had faith and was praying receives a financial windfall in the nick of time to save her home. 1 John 5:14-15 says, *"And this is the confidence that we have in him, that, if we ask anything according to his will; He heareth us: And if we know that he hear us, whatsoever we ask, we know that we have the petitions that we desire of him."* So, we know he hears us when we have faith and pray and believe we shall have it.

In addition, John 15:7 says, *"If ye abide in me, and my words abide in you, ye shall ask what ye will, and it shall be done unto you."* The Bible says sometimes God provides miracles, large and small, in order to do his own will, such as a child being born, and souls being saved. Hebrews 2:4 says, *"God also bearing them witness, both with signs and wonders, and with divers miracles, and gifts of the Holy Ghost, according to his own will."* I often wonder about the changing temperature of Hallie's headstone after the visit from Charlie Jones. I wonder if this is one of those things God put into place simply to make sure that when the time came to execute His plan for me, I would be *Paying Attention?* It's obvious that the heat in the stone was something from within me; I was the only one feeling it, and the snow still sat on the cold stone just like any other rock and did not melt away. I think it was because the Holy Spirit was teaching me even then, although I did not recognize it was there. Yet another 0316 verse, 1 Corinthians 3:16, says, *"Know ye are not that ye are the temple of God, and that the Spirit of God dwelleth in you?"* I believe Charlie delivered the required message and the need for my attention there was now fulfilled, so the heat in the stone became the heat in me, transferred as to make it easy for me to not be lukewarm but be on fire for the Lord. A small miracle perhaps? It was a mystery for certain.

The rings Charlie used to pay for his drink are a mystery as well. There are many mentions of rings in the Bible, mostly signet rings used to make one's mark, like a signature, in biblical times. They were a status symbol mostly and a way to do secure commerce with the right people, a way for kings to seal documents and powerful men to seal written orders. Rings were also given as gifts on occasion as a reward for loyalty. Because Charlie first gave two rings, it could be a symbol of unity as in a marriage, but there are so many two's in the Bible, it is hard to pin down. There are two parts of the Bible, the Old and New Testaments, Jesus sent the disciples out two by two, the word *God* appears in all books except two: Esther and the Song of Solomon. God created two lights, and the shortest verse in the Bible, John 11:35, has only two words: *"Jesus wept."* Genesis 19:1 tells of two angels sent to Sodom, and Luke 16:13 says, *"No servant can serve two masters: for either he will hate the one, and love the other; or else he will hold to the one, and despise the other. Ye cannot serve God and mammon."*

Then Charlie left an additional ring, now a total of three. This is the number of completeness, the trinity is three, Jonah was in the whale for three days and three nights, and of course the most obvious: Jesus was in the grave three days and three nights. So, with all the twos, threes, and rings in the Bible, there must be some connection, but for now, the rings meaning remain another mystery.

There are also other numbers in the Bible and in my personal testimony that make me notice them and wonder why they are, what they are, and what future meaning they may have. Other things remain a *mystery* as well, such as why Terrye Clear had his dream on the day I was saved, a connection of some kind exists there; the trail numbers Charlie traveled to get from Iron City to Winfield; and the name of Hallie's grandmother having the same name as Glenna. Is there a connection between the Donahue name and the Dannenhauer name? Who was the woman who apparently could also see Charlie at the cemetery in Winfield but would not speak with me? Did she know the mystery? Will I ever know what or who Charlie is or was? Was he real, a vision, or a messenger sent in a form I would believe and relate to perhaps?

I cannot help but think Charlie opened a door, enabling me to be rid of my alcoholism right then and there, the first time we meant. I had to do the work, of course. Then I was given the time necessary for this testimony to unfold. It was a test to see if I could and would believe in Jesus Christ. I could, and I did. The fact that I am alive at all and am sober is by the grace of God. The *mystery* must be that I am still here; for some reason, God is not done with me. Remember there are many *mysteries* we are not meant to understand now but will be revealed to us when its God's time as we understand His Word more fully. John 8:32 says, *"And ye shall know the truth, and the truth shall make you free."*

Chapter 13
DO IT NOW

THE QUESTIONS ARE MANY, AND THE answers are few. I do know for sure that when my journey started at the beginning of this book, all these things were truly a mystery to me. As I am learning, and I hope you are beginning to see, it was a mystery to me how my life could become so difficult and confusing. I was a good man by most standards, I worked hard, I was faithful to my wife, and I was good to those around me. I didn't lie, cheat, or steal. I even believed in God, but the mystery totally escaping me was that I was living my life outside the will of God. I did not know Jesus Christ as my Savior, placing all the importance on things of the world: money, possessions, and status. I am certain this is why there are so many references to the mystery in the Bible.

I put myself before others, and without even realizing it, I committed the seven deadly sins against God every day. These were natural tendencies given to me and to each one of us by God to enable us to navigate through this life and live in a Christ-like manner. They had gone astray in me as they have in most of us due to sin, perceived uniqueness caused once good, God given traits to go rampantly astray. This caused me to live in total ignorance of the way I needed to live and most generally in the opposite way I should have been living. I was a showoff, totally in pride, wanting to be the standout in any circumstance, even at the expense of those I cared about. Proverbs 29:23 says, "*A man's pride shall bring him low: but honor shall uphold the humble spirit.*" Now, I give the glory to God.

Greed creeps into our lives and helps us to justify "bending the rules," like cheating on our taxes, abusing the charity system in our society, and taking advantage when the opportunity presents itself, especially when money is involved. 1 Timothy 6:10 says, "*For the love of money is the root of all evil: which while some coveted after, they erred from the faith, and pierced themselves through with many sorrows.*" Now, do not misunderstand; we must earn, have, and use money every day as a means of survival. It is the *love* of money that I avoid. I use it like a tool, like a hammer drives a nail; money is provided by the grace of God to get the things we need to survive take care of our own and follow God's word.

Lust is the overwhelming desire for anything exceeding the desire for God, power, money, sex, literally anything. We can watch a bird fly over and notice it, but to let it build a nest on our head is lust. In other words, it is okay to notice these things, but to embrace and dwell on them is lustful and wrong. Galatians 5:16 says, "*This I say then, walk in the Spirit, and ye shall not fulfil the lust of the flesh.*" The more I train my brain to see the things I once lusted after and not dwell on them, the easier and more blessed my life becomes by the grace of God.

Wrath, violent uncontrolled anger, is sin that causes domestic violence, bar fights, family disputes, even wars and a majority of other disturbances; all of which are evil. The devil loves this because he knows where the chinks in our armor are, where to push our button, and he does. It is about controlling our reaction to outside forces as this is the only thing we can control ourselves, with God's help. Ephesians 4:26-27 says, "*Be ye angry, and sin not: let not the sun go down on thy wrath: Neither give place to the devil.*" Wrath seems to come to the surface in us with a vengeance when by some occasion, our particularly sinful nature is brought to our attention. We know deep down that life is accusing of us something that we are fully guilty of; it is indefensible in rational or biblical terms, so the explosion of our wrath is ignited for lack of any other way to justify our actions.

Covetousness is another sin. What a world we live in; an ad comes on the television, shows us a product, and we want it simply because someone else has one. We have no need for whatever it is; we simply want it because it's there, no reason, just want, want, want. Hebrews 13:5 says, *"Let your conversation be without covetousness; and be content with such things as ye have: for he hath said, I will never leave thee, nor forsake thee."* If we need something, God, through the mystery of Jesus Christ, will make sure we have it.

Envy is wanting what others have. I wanted the money, recognition, and possessions of others; anything that was better than what I already had, I wanted it. Not only did I want it, but I wanted to take it from them so I could have it. Proverbs 14:30 says, *"A sound heart is the life of the flesh: but envy the rottenness of the bones."* Now, through these biblical teachings, I have learned to be content with the worldly possessions God has given to me, as all things belong to God, and I am just a steward. I am humbled by what I have and know that I will have what I need every day simply by God's grace.

Gluttony, I always wanted "all I could get" even if it meant me having more that I needed and someone else having less than they needed, whether money, food, or booze. I always had to have more than I needed, and I consumed it like wildfire. Proverbs 23:21 says, *"For the drunkard and the Glutton shall come to poverty: and drowsiness shall clothe a man with rags."* Boy, did this happen to me, literally. I now strive to have enough, but many times when someone I know needs help, I help even if it may cause my household to scrape and scrimp, not because I want recognition or reward, but just because scripture says we as Christians should do this.

Sloth is taking more than one gives to whomever or whatever is being taken from by simple lack of trying, not the inability to participate or help but having the ability and choosing not to help when able to; it's simple laziness. We all do this, some more than others, not taking away from those who need help in any way, as many do. 2 Thessalonians 3:10 says, *"For even when we were with you, this we commanded you, that if any would not work, neither should he eat."* To combat this, my goal is to always do my part, and then do more to the best of my ability. God knows what is in our heart, as in 1 Samuel 16:7, it says, *"But the Lord said unto Samuel, Look not on his countenance, or on the height of his stature; because I have refused him: for the Lord seeth not as a man seeth; for man looketh on the outward appearance, but the Lord looketh on the heart."*

Before the things that have been described in this book happened, I was mentally coasting through life. I took what I wanted and left the rest for someone else to figure out. Because no man had shown me spiritual things, I had no idea God was there, or cared that He had sent His only son to die on a cross for our sin and to give us everlasting life. I had heard about it, but it was of no concern to me, until my spiritual awakening through learning to *"Pay Attention"*. Now, I understand that even this condition I was in was biblical. 1 Corinthians 2:14 says, *"But the natural man receiveth not the things of the spirit of God: for they are foolishness unto him: neither can he know them, because they are spiritually discerned."* I was simply unable to understand the mystery. I don't know what causes any one to have a spiritual awakening; perhaps a traumatic experience, near death experience, loss of a loved one, financial collapse, addiction, health issues, and many others have all been pointed to. I believe it all boils down to the idea that at some point in life, we finally have a small glimpse of the presence of God because for whatever reason, at that moment in time, our heart was open, and we were *Paying Attention.* This always happens when we least expect it and always at the perfect time in our life when we are ready, no sooner and no later. God's timing is always perfect. I can only speak for myself, and this is exactly what happened to me. I needed help; I needed Jesus, and I knew I was seeking Him. I asked Him to save me, and because my heart was open and I was *Paying Attention*, He saved me. The Holy spirit entered me and indwelled me, and the mystery had happened in my life.

It does not matter where you are right now in life. You could have been saved for a week or a decade or a century, but if deep down in your heart, you don't understand the mystery and are not receiving the full blessings available to all believers, then you may have fallen away. Luke 8:13 says, *"They on the rock are they, which when they hear, receive the word with joy; and these have no root, which for a while believe, and in time of temptation fall away."* Or perhaps you believe you are just not good enough; your sins are just so bad that Jesus Christ would never forgive someone like you. The good news is you are wrong. The Apostle Paul was the worst sinner ever. When he found Jesus, he was on his way to capture, torture and kill still more Christians, and Jesus came into his open heart and saved him. He became one of the most prolific teachers of the gospel, ever. This is not about who you were or who you are; it's about who you want to be, and salvation is there for all who seek God, confess their sins, and ask for forgiveness. Everyone can do this.

This chapter title, *Do It Now,* would indicate some sense of urgency. We all know deep down what not to do day-to-day, moment-to-moment; we call it guilt or hollowness. We know what wrong is, and we can know what feels bad in our hearts.

There is no doubt when we do wrong. So, I hope and pray this book has given you a glimpse into how to *Pay Attention* to that little voice way down inside, the good voice that is the Holy Spirit, the whisper of God, who opens a window wide open to eternity in heaven through Jesus Christ, the Son of God. Yes, you have heard that voice before; you probably remember exactly when and where. Job 4:12 says, *"Now a thing was secretly brought to me, and mine ear received a little thereof."*

Perhaps you listened, perhaps you did not, but I am certain you have heard it. You knew you heard it; you probably wanted to hear it clearly but were not sure how. God is everywhere. He is here right now with me, and He is there right now with you. If you choose to not listen, He still loves you and will be there when you decide to *Pay Attention* and listen. One of the mysteries is how this communication works for me and I pray it works for you. If you want relief from your strife, your guilt, your trouble in this life, simply *Pay Attention* enough to hear the whisper. Psalm 31:24 says, *"Be of good courage, and he shall strengthen your heart, all ye that hope in the Lord,"* Just enough to allow Jesus Christ to come into your heart and accept him as your Savior.

The communication will begin immediately. Prayer will give you an open line of communication to the greatest power ever. God does answer prayer, so once the line of communication is open and you accept Him as your Savior, the Bible makes it very clear that He hears our prayers. 1 John 5:14-15 says, *"And this is the confidence that we have in him, that if we ask anything according to his will, he heareth us. And if we know that he hear us, whatsoever we ask, we know that we have the petitions that we desire of him."* Jesus Himself said in Mark 11:24 saying, *"Therefore I say unto you, What things soever ye desire, when ye pray, believe that you receive them, and ye shall have them."*

So now you know, the *mystery* is here for the understanding, right here in front of you written in these pages. James 4:8 says, *"Draw nigh to God, and he will draw nigh to you. Cleanse your hands, ye sinners; and purify your hearts, ye double minded."* When you open your heart to Jesus and understand the love He has for you and let Him save you and move closer to Him, He will move closer to you as well, and suddenly He will be doing things for you that you can't do for yourself. Matthew 7:78 says, *"Ask, and it shall be given you; seek and ye shall find; knock, and it shall be opened unto you, For everyone that asketh receiveth; and he that seeketh findeth; and to him that knocketh it shall be opened."*

Now the seed has planted, and if you wish, you can put this book down and never look at it again; you can throw it in the trash and walk away, thinking I am crazy. You can ignore the mystery if you choose to, for now perhaps. But all will serve the Lord; we have no choice in the matter. Romans 14:11 says, *"For it is written, As I live, saith the Lord, every knee shall bow to me, every tongue shall confess to God."* So, the message has been delivered. Revelation 3:20 says, *"Behold, I stand at the door, and knock: if any man hear my voice, and open the door, I will come into him, and will sup with him, and he with me."* I pray you are *Paying Attention* and act.

The Bible also tells us it is wrong to continue in our sinful ways after we have received this knowledge, and you have heard it now. The question is, were you *Paying Attention* enough to hear and receive the good news? I pray you are, you did, or at the very least you want to. Hebrews 10:26 says, *"For if we sin willfully after that we have received the knowledge of the truth, there remaineth no more sacrifice for sins."*

The choice is yours. Isaiah 40:31 says, *"But they that wait upon the LORD shall renew their strength; they shall mount up with wings as eagles; they shall run, and not be weary; and they shall walk and not faint."*

RESOURCES

HOPE THAT BY THE TIME YOU ARE reading this, you just got finished reading *Pay Attention*. Should you be one of those who has an addiction and are feeling motivated to do something about it, I want the information to be at your fingertips. Or, if you are a person who knows someone who may need some help, I want that to be available as well. I think I could list hundreds of places to get help for drugs, alcohol, gambling, sex, or any other addiction that lurks out there. The same would apply for support groups for all the above and more. A simple list will not motivate anyone to get the help they need any more than the lack of a list will stop someone who really wants to get help from finding it. Use the same determination to get help you need and want that you used to get the next fix.

Resources include the internet, your doctor, clergy, family, and friends. The possibilities where one might find the initial motivation are endless, perhaps in this book. The one thing I will recommend over all of these is the Bible (Basic Instructions Before Leaving Earth). The answers are in that holiest of books, no matter what the problem is; all that is needed is willingness to start. Aristotle said, "Well begun is half done," so the most important thing is to get started and realize that God loves us all. He tells us in Romans 8:31, "*What shall we say to these things, if God be for us, who can be against us?"* We tend to make things harder than they really are. Stephen Hawking said, *"I believe things cannot make themselves impossible."* I believe this to be true. The same holds true of anyone reading this, who just wants to be free. Start now right now, make that decision, commit to it, and remember the journey around the world begins with that first step. Take it now. Pray for help and God will answer.

SCRIPTURE READINGS

The ten commandments found in Exodus 20.

3, *Thou shalt have no other gods before me.*

4-6, *Thou shalt not make unto thee any graven image, nor any likeness of anything that is in heaven above, or that is in earth beneath, or that is in the water under the earth: Thou shalt not bow down thyself to them, nor serve them: for I the Lord thy God am a jealous God, visiting the iniquity of the fathers upon the children unto the third and fourth generation of them who hate me; And shewing mercy unto thousands of them that love me, and keep my commandments.*

7, *Thou shalt not take the name of the Lord thy God in vein; for the Lord will not hold him guiltless that taketh his name in vain.*

8-11, *Remember the sabbath day, to keep it holy. Six days thou shalt labour, and do all thy work: But the seventh day is the sabbath of the Lord thy God: in it thou shalt not do any work, though nor thy son, nor thy daughter, thy manservant, nor thy maidservant, nor thy cattle, nor thy stranger that is within your gates: For in six days the Lord made heaven and earth, the sea, and all that in them is, and rested the seventh day: wherefor the Lord blessed the sabbath day, and hallowed it.*

12, *Honor thy father and thy mother: that thy days may be long upon the land which the Lord thy God giveth thee.*

13, *Thou shalt not kill.*

14, *Thou shalt not commit adultery.*

15, *Thou shalt not steal.*

16, *Thou shalt not bear false witness against thy neighbor.*

17, *Thou shalt not covet thy neighbor's house, thou shalt not covet thy neighbor's wife, nor his manservant, nor his maidservant, nor his ox, nor his ass, nor any thing that is thy neighbor's.*

Matthew 23:

13, *But woe unto you, scribes and Pharisees, hypocrites! for ye shut up the kingdom of heaven against men: for ye neither go in yourselves, neither suffer ye them that are entering to go in.*

14, *Woe unto you, scribes and Pharisees, hypocrites! for ye devour widows' houses, and for a pretense make long prayer: therefor ye shall receive the greater damnation.*

15, *Woe unto you, scribes and Pharisees, hypocrites! for ye compass sea and land to make one proselyte, and when he is made, ye make him two-fold more the child of hell than yourselves.*

16, *Woe unto you, ye blind guides, which say, whosoever shall swear by the temple, it is nothing; but whosoever shall swear by the gold of the temple, he is a debtor.*

23, *Woe unto you, scribes and Pharisees, hypocrites! for ye pay tithe of mint and anise and cumin, and have omitted the weightier matters of the law, judgment, mercy, and faith: these ought ye to have done, and not to leave the other undone.*

25, *Woe unto you, scribes and Pharisees, hypocrites! for ye make clean the outside of the cup and of the platter, but within they are full of extortion and excess.*

27, *Woe unto you, scribes and Pharisees, hypocrites! for ye are like whited sepulchers, which indeed appear beautiful outward, but are within full of dead men's bones, and of all uncleanness.*

29-30, *Woe unto you, scribes and Pharisees, hypocrites! because ye build the tombs of the prophets, and garnish the sepulchers of the righteous, And say, If we had been in the days of our fathers, we would not have been partakers with them in the blood of the prophets.*

Hebrews 11, faith defines and exemplified.

1, *Now faith is the substance of things hoped for, the evidence of things not seen.*

2, *For by it the elders obtained a good report.*

3, *Through faith we understand that the words were framed by the word of God, so that things which are seen were not made of things which do appear.*

4, *By faith Abel offered unto God a more excellent sacrifice than Cain, by which he obtained witness that he was righteous, God testifying of his gifts: and by it he being dead yet speaketh.*

5, *By faith Enoch was translated that he should not see death; and was not found, because God had translated him: for before his translation he had this testimony that he pleased God.*

6, *But without faith it is impossible to please him: for he that cometh God must believe that he is, and that he is a rewarder of them that diligently seek him.*

7, *By faith Noah, being warned of God of things not seen as yet, moved with fear, prepared an ark to the saving of his house; by the which he condemned the world, and became heir of the righteousness which is by faith.*

8, *By faith Abraham, when he was called to go out into a place which he should after receive for an inheritance, obeyed; and he went out, not knowing whither he went.*

9, *By faith he sojourned in the land of promise, as in a strange country, dwelling in tabernacles with Isaac and Jacob, the heirs with him of the same promise.*

10, *For he looked for a city which hath foundations, whose builder and maker is God.*

11, *Through faith also Sara herself received strength to conceive seed, and was delivered a child when she was past age, because she judged him faithful who had promised.*

12, *Therefor sprang there even of one, and him as good as dead, so many as the starts of the sky in multitude, and as the sand which is by the sea shore innumerable.*

13, *These all died in faith, not having received the promises, but having seen them afar off, and were persuaded of them and embraced them, and confessed that they were strangers and pilgrims on the earth.*

14, *For they say such things declare plainly that they seek a country.*

15, *And truly, if they had been mindful of that country from whence they came out, they might have had opportunity to have returned.*

16, *But now they desire a better country, that is, an heavenly: Wherefore God is not ashamed to be called their God: for he hath prepared for them a city.*

17, *By faith Abraham, when he was tried, offered up Isaac: and he that had received the promises offered up his only begotten son,*

18, *Of whom it was said, That in Isaac shall thy seed be called:*

19, *Accounting that God was to raise him up, even from the dead; from whence also received him in a figure.*

20, *By faith Isaac blessed Jacob and Esau concerning things to come.*

21, *By Faith Jacob, when he was a dying, blessed both the sons of Joseph; and worshipped, leaning upon the top of his staff.*

22, *By faith Joseph, when he died, made mention of the departing of the children of Israel; and gave commandment concerning his bones.*

23, *By faith Moses, when he was born, was hid three months of his parents, because they saw he was a proper child; and they were not afraid of the kings commandment.*

24, *By faith Moses, when he was come to years, refused to be called the son of Pharaoh's daughter;*

25, *Choosing rather to suffer affliction with the people of God, than to enjoy the pleasures of sin for a season;*

26, *Esteeming the reproach of Christ greater riches than the treasures in Egypt: for he had respect unto the recompence of the reward.*

27, *By faith he forsook Egypt, not fearing the wrath of the king: for he endured, as seeing him who is invisible.*

28, *Through faith he kept the Passover, and the sprinkling of the blood, lest he that destroyed the firstborn should touch them.*

29, *By faith they passed through the Red sea as by dry land: which the Egyptians assaying to do were drowned*

30, *By faith the walls of Jericho fell down, after they were compassed about seven days.*

31, *By faith the harlot Rahab perished not with them that believed not, when she had received the spies with peace.*

32, *And what shall I more say? For the time would fail me to tell of Gideon, and of Barak, and of Samson, and of Jephthae; of David also, and Samuel, and of the prophets:*

33, *Who through faith subdued kingdoms, wrought righteousness, obtained promises, stopped the mouths of lions,*

34, *Quenched the violence of fire, escaped the edge of the sword, out of weakness were made strong, waxed valiant in fight, turned to flight the armies of aliens.*

35, *Women received their dead raised to life again: and others were tortured, not accepting deliverance; that they might obtain a better resurrection:*

36, *And others had trial of cruel mockings and scouragings, yea, moreover of bonds and imprisonment:*

37, *They were stoned, they were sawn asunder, were tempted, were slain with the sword: they wandered about in sheepskins and goatskins; being destitute, afflicted, tormented;*

38, *(Of whom the world was not worthy:) they wandered in deserts, and in the mountains, and in dens and caves of the earth.*

39, *And these all, having obtained a good report through faith, received not the promise:*

40, *God having provided some better thing for us, that they without us should not be made perfect.*

I AM WILLIAM A. DONAHUE (BILL), BORN in Pueblo, Colorado, on March 13, 1960, to William A. Donahue (deceased) and Janet L. Donahue (deceased). I am the second child of three, making me a middle child, one older brother, Jeff (two years older, living), one younger sister, Christy (eight years younger, deceased). I have been married to Sheila Joe Donahue (Tucker) of Missoula, Montana, for four years. I am five feet, eight inches tall, 180 pounds, plus or minus. I am gray and balding now but in good health. I was raised in a small mountain town called Beulah in the mountains of southern Colorado. There is nothing special about me, with just an ordinary childhood and teenage years much the same. Early on, I developed into a hard-working, honest person. The only higher education I had, other than the school of hard knocks, was lots of hands-on experience.

I married at nineteen to a short-time sweetheart (Kim) and divorced after a decade, with one daughter (Chelsea Megan Donahue). I worked several different jobs, eventually starting and running my own business in the late '80s. Then came the 1991 marriage to Glenna Sue Donahue (Ward), and I remained with her until her death in 2016. This is the time frame the book began to take form, unknown to me, it was just life. The point is, I was just an ordinary guy living an ordinary life in an ordinary place with all the ordinary problems we all have as we go through life. I had a case of terminal uniqueness by the time this testimony began to unfold, thinking I was special and had control of everything and everyone around me.

I am just a garden variety human being. I played the part well, and my addiction to alcohol was my main cheerleader in it all. As with many people, my life, through my own arrogance and poor decision making had begun to unravel. The testimony in the book you just read is why I am still alive to write this today. The relationship I have been blessed enough to develop with God is why I am now realizing I am in control of nothing. It brings a clear look forward that the real reason I am here is to serve my Savior, Jesus Christ, as best I can with the tools I have. So, this book is just a glimpse into me, an ordinary fellow living now for a much-higher power, God. The reason this book got written at all was because ever so slowly, one small bite at a time, I learned to *Pay Attention*.